CN00665075

The Survival Guide To Staying Conscious

BURGS

About The Author

Originally from the UK, Burgs began his meditation practice in Asia, initially as an assistant for the famous Indonesian healer and meditation teacher Merta Ada. He went on to practice meditation under the guidance of some of the greatest living Buddhist meditation masters, with HH Dodrupchen Rinpoche and Pa Auk Sayadaw as his principal teachers. He spent many years doing intensive self-practice under the guidance of his teachers in both India and Burma where he ordained as a monk, to be personally tutored and trained by Pa Auk Sayadaw. On completion of his training, during which he practiced to the highest levels of Jhana concentration, he disrobed in order to bring what he had learned to a Western audience within the context of a lay life. He was recognised by his teachers as having unusual depth of practice and ability and began teaching at their request.

He first held retreat in 1996 and has since hosted over a hundred retreats, from 5 days to 5 months in length, and has taught thousands of people from all walks of life. His students have ranged from total beginners to distinguished monks and nuns, from the homeless of Asia to some of Europe's most successful and influential businessmen.

He has a rare ability to communicate deep knowledge of meditation and the mechanics and functioning of consciousness with a clarity that has been greatly appreciated by Western audiences, making him an extremely accessible teacher. Today he is one of the most experienced and accomplished meditation teachers in the West.

Burgs is the author of a number of books including Beyond the Veil and the Flavour of Liberation Series, with the Flavour of Liberation now recognised internationally as a leading commentary on the practice and mechanics of meditation. He lives simply in the Pyrenees where he is building a model of sustainable community life. He remains deeply committed to exploring the effects that both modern technology and lifestyle is having upon the integrity of our consciousness.

For further information about Burgs
and The Art of Meditation please visit
theartofmeditation.org

Other books by the author

Beyond the Veil *(Autobiography)*

The Flavour of Liberation Volume One & Two:
*Healing Transformation through Meditation
and The Practice of Jhana*

The Flavour of Liberation Volume Three:
*The Practice of Vipassana and The Path to
the Deathless State*

Acknowledgements

Compiling a book that is as current as this is not without its challenges, both because the content itself is challenging and because things are changing so quickly. It has often been necessary to reframe some of the context in light of how I have seen people responding on a month by month basis to the extraordinary pace at which these changes are happening. So it has taken great perseverance from the editing team to keep pace with the content and bring it to the final draft.

I am deeply grateful to the editor Hugo Sandon, for his tireless efforts and patience with my constant amendments. Without his contribution I think it is fair to say this book could well still be a work in progress. A huge thank you also to Miranda Acland and Katie St. George who have worked hard to turn my spoken word into something grammatically acceptable and legible. Not an easy job I am sure! Thank you also to Ben Dias, George Pickford and Andy Raingold, all of whom have contributed.

I am forever grateful for the team of volunteers and assistants who help me at every level to bring these teachings to an ever wider audience.

August 2016

For more information please visit
www.theartofmeditation.org

ISBN 9780956891761

Brave Souls

There is an album called Brave Souls which accompanies this book. It contains a number of inspirational audio tracks combining original discourses from Burgs' retreat with music written by a range of amazing musicians. The hope is that the album adds an element of direct transmission and connection to the heart essence of the teachings that have formed the basis for this book. Included in this book are references to various album tracks that relate to the topics being explored here.

CONTENTS

Part Three: A Give Back Generation

Part One:

More To Life Than Meets The Eye

1

Life's Deep Mystery

"For it is in giving that we receive."
- Saint Francis of Assisi

I think there's a little part of everybody that has an inkling, a hunch, a sense that there's a mystery in the background behind this life that we haven't quite clocked and we'd love to know what's going on.

In the deepest part of us there is clearly a sense that there's more to life than meets the eye. No matter how hard we've tried to break life down into the nuts and bolts and say, "Well, this is what it is", honestly, we have to admit that life is an extraordinary mystery. And anyone trying to rob it of that mystery and insisting on understanding what's going on, I think, is probably missing the juiciest part of it, the part that makes it feel that life is really something worth getting stuck into.

There's an awful lot of drudgery in life, there's a lot of things we have to do that are inconvenient, there's a lot of hardship. Life isn't easy. And yet the desire for life, the 'longing' for it, remains *so* strong. Even in the face of extraordinary adversity the longing for life is still there.

If we look out into nature, everywhere we look

- apart from where we have put something - there's life just pouring forth, and it has this extraordinary, inexorable, unstoppable-ness about it. This boundless power of life is working through us too, we are a part of that, we're an expression of it, we *are* that. That mysterious power that is driving all life is there within us, twenty-four hours of every day, and although we distract ourselves so desperately and spend most of our time really distracted from what's actually going on, somewhere inside of us there's a knowing or a hunch that there's clearly more to this than we might have thought.

And yet with this astonishingly beautiful display of life going on around us endlessly, it seems more and more of us, if we are truly honest with ourselves, feel deep down that something is not quite right about the way we relate to life itself.

In this book I hope to take you on a journey deep into the very heart of the mystery that is life. By looking a little more deeply at what is actually going on in the background, as a society and as humans on this planet, we might re-establish a healthier and more enriching relationship to the life that each of us is a part.

I would like to encourage you to look at life with an open and honest mind and a courageous heart, so that we might reach a place of deep reverence and respect for it and not fall into the tendency of taking it for granted or assuming it will always be there. It is rare indeed and most precious. I believe that only once we have rediscovered the sense of awe and wonder at life will we develop a more healthy attitude towards it. This attitude will form the backbone and bedrock of not just our own welfare, but that of the generations to come.

Life Is Too Precious To Not Pay Attention

If we can learn to really pay attention to what is going on within us and around us, life itself becomes our perfect teacher. If we are willing to recognise it, life is showing us what it is we need to do all the time. There is an innate intelligence at work behind our lives which is reflected at all times in everything that we experience. It is my hope that this book will help you to come to a deeper understanding of that intelligence and ultimately point to a way in which we can start to live more in alignment with it. Maybe it's been going on beyond our perception and conscious understanding, but still, deep down, some part of us knows.

My simple aspiration for this book is to offer hope and a signpost to a wholly positive approach to the predicament that we face as human beings, alive at this very extraordinary time. I wish to propose a solution, which is for all of us to collectively become part of what I call the Give Back Generation, a generation who seek to contribute to the world more than we take from it. In fifty years from now, history will testify to how we chose to meet our challenges. Those who will follow in our wake will live through the outcome of the choices we have made.

During his life twenty-five centuries ago the Buddha[1] often spoke of an age of degeneration when beings lose their moral compass and become obsessed solely with selfish pursuits at great detriment to themselves, others and the world in which they live. Although I do not propose to look at life from a fixed Buddhist perspective in this book, as human beings alive today we still face the same propensity to create

---

1 **Gautama Buddha**, also known as **Siddhārtha Gautama**, **Shakyamuni Buddha**, or simply the **Buddha**, was an ascetic and sage on whose teachings **Buddhism** was founded. He is believed to have lived and taught mostly in the eastern part of the Indian sub-continent sometime between the sixth and fourth centuries BCE.

suffering in our lives and so his teachings remain as relevant today as they did back then.

Below is a list of the five signs of degeneration of consciousness that the Buddha identified. At this point all I wish to do is to simply flag these points up and just encourage you to see if you have noticed some of these things yourself in the world around you. They are listed here so that you can use them as a guide or a point of reference to the suggestions made in the book that follows, nothing more. It is not my intention at this stage to seek to support or negate these claims, but merely to frame our own investigation of human consciousness and inform how we can best take care of it.

The Degeneration of Time: the quality of things deteriorates, food becomes less nutritious, grain tastes less good and does not ripen, the environment becomes degraded, famine and wars proliferate, and new diseases arise.

The Degeneration of Disturbing Emotions: the virtue of householders declines, negative emotions proliferate, self-obsession proliferates to the point where pride, competitiveness and greed become so embedded that beings find it almost impossible to surmount them.

The Degeneration of Views: wrong views proliferate; beings cannot see what is happening to them and reject the truth when it is spoken, they tend to believe in wrong philosophies and find it hard to believe in right view. They reject the law of cause and effect believing the idea of Karma[2] to be mere superstition as they assume themselves not to be accountable for their actions. This becomes the cause for a gradual degeneration of behaviour and moral integrity and people become more and more driven by desire with no ethical restraint upon that desire. Assuming that it is OK to do whatever they want regardless of consequences people develop attitudes that are morally degenerate, and become intolerant to the point of hatred.

The Degeneration of Physical Form: degeneration of appearance, obesity proliferates, intellect degenerates, good health degenerates, beings become harder to help and harder to subdue.

The Degeneration of the Life Span: afflictive conditions proliferate and gradually the life span shortens.

At times such as these the choices that beings make will determine their welfare or suffering.

So having read the above, each and every one of you can make your own reflections as to whether or not you see in the world around you now emotions, views, physical forms and life spans degenerating or regenerating. There will be pockets where this is happening at different rates.

---

2   I do not wish to engage in a lengthy discussion of karma in this book as I am aware that it is sometimes a contentious subject and it is often misunderstood, rejected etc., particularly in the West. Karma means the energy behind our action, and actually refers to our volition, desire, will or intention. As such, while subtle, it is a real aspect of our conscious experience. The Buddha said "It is volition that is karma; having willed I act" i.e it is the volition or intention behind our actions that is karma. I will explain in more detail how it functions within our consciousness in a later chapter.

Yet at the macro level, there is no doubt in my mind which way we are heading. Barring the fact we are all living longer lives due to huge advances in health care, I see all the other signs of degeneration proliferating, often at alarming rates. It is up to you to decide on your own position, but please be honest with yourselves, don't sell yourself short. Because our aspiration is hopefully not to alarm ourselves but to stand tall in the search for solutions.

I cannot put it any more eloquently or succinctly than *Charles Eisenstein* in his book *The More Beautiful World Our Hearts Know is Possible*:

"Who would have foreseen, two generations ago when the story of progress was strong, that the twenty-first century would be the time of school massacres, of rampant obesity, of growing indebtedness, of pervasive insecurity, of intensifying concentration of wealth, of unabated world hunger, and of environmental degradation that threatens civilization? The world was supposed to be getting better. We were supposed to be becoming wealthier, more enlightened. Society was supposed to be advancing...

Why do the visions of a more beautiful world that seemed so close in the middle twentieth century now seem so unreachable that all we can hope for is to survive in an ever more competitive, ever more degraded world? Truly, our stories have failed us. Is it too much to ask, to live in a world where our human gifts go toward the benefit of all? Where our daily activities contribute to the healing of the biosphere and the well-being of other people?"

The paradox to this is that if we were able to truly see what is happening to us and fully understand the way of things, there is no way that we would be living life the way we are. Perhaps the problem has been that we somehow have managed to convince ourselves that these signs of degeneration are happening out there in the world beyond us, but not been willing to look at what is actually happening *to* us. Well, sadly, what we see going on in the world around us *is* a reflection of what is going on within us.

So what would happen to us if we did fully understand what we were doing and the implications of it? Of these five signs which the Buddha described that mark the coming of an age of degeneration, one of them is that beings reject the truth even when it is put in front of them. The truth in the end is right in front of us every day if we were only willing to see it. The question is - are we willing to pay attention?

Not enough people in positions of responsibility and power are telling us we have to consume less, give more to others and share what we have. It is almost as if no one dares to deliver the inconvenient truth that would give us the wake up call we need to become galvanized. "Don't worry, technology will provide a solution", is the most common response I hear from people these days when discussing the apparent and potential problems that are staring us in the face.

This unwillingness to address the challenges we face in many ways is understandable. I am sure it is not just indolence, although that no doubt plays a part. Fear will also be prompting us to pretend that these things just aren't happening, or hope that somehow they will all just go away on their own. But we all know that closing our eyes and pretending that the burglar isn't there doesn't stop him making off with all our possessions.

But I feel there is another equally important reason for us not addressing the issues we face. And that is that somehow we have lost sight or lost touch with how truly precious and sacred life actually is. We consider our survival as humans, at whatever cost, to be more important than the sanctity and integrity of the life we sustain. For one reason or another, we have gradually removed the sense of sacred from almost everything in our lives these days. Life itself is no longer seen as something sacred. It has become commodified. For decades now the assumption has been that life is a material and mechanical process within which consciousness is a by-product. But have we stopped to ask whether it might be the case that the alarming increase in depression and hopelessness that so many otherwise fortunate human beings are experiencing these days might actually be because they lack that very spiritual context to their lives that makes it feel truly special? Or that we have stopped seeing life itself as sacred?

While we may initially think what we need are tools by which to cope better with life as it is, the fact that we aren't coping so well with the lives we are living is a sign that we may be off track. Learning to cope with being unwell is in no way as satisfactory or complete a resolution as recovering from our affliction. At a deeper level many of us are longing to find a higher sense of meaning while questioning the actual direction we are heading in. Real change is what so many of us today are actually looking for, while what we are being offered are tools by which we can cope well enough to stay on the trajectory we are on. In truth we do not need help staying on course. What we need is encouragement to embrace a sea change.

I have little doubt that there are countless people out there just waiting for permission to embrace a quantum change of direction. Experience suggests that deep and profound change tends only to happen when it is thrust upon us. The problem with this is that forced change inevitably brings with it far more suffering and hardship than when we make choices for ourselves consciously.

A slap in the face with a wet fish, though unpleasant, is not nearly as difficult to live with as being knocked off your feet with the ground giving way beneath you. Indeed, if it serves to wake us up before we fall asleep at the wheel, it has served an important purpose. So I am sure we are all better served by honestly looking into the predicament we are in and digging deep in search of solutions, rather than just trying to convince ourselves that everything is going to be all right.

The Future Is In Our Hands

The further out of alignment with the truth behind our lives we become, the more inconvenient that truth feels. If we resent the suggestion that we need to change, it is usually not just because it is inconvenient, but because it interferes with our personal aspirations and the pursuit of our goals and desires.

When I left my last teacher in India, at the end of years of intensive training in meditation and yoga, his final request to me was to return home and to continue to meditate for the benefit of others. Over the years many people have come on retreat to learn meditation, and almost all of them come hoping that meditation will in some way enrich their lives. At the end of every retreat, I explain two basic principles that our welfare and progress in the future stand upon.

The first principle is that if you are going to continue to centre your life around the pursuit of your desires, you will need to be totally unwilling to harm others or yourself in the pursuit of those desires if you are to safeguard your well-being in the long term.

The second principle is that if we expect to be able to take out more than we put in, it is a certainty that over time the quality of life will degenerate, because however abundant our planet is, it is not infinite in its capacity to provide.

It may take more than a brief glance at these statements to grasp what they are truly saying. They are, in effect, nothing more than expressions of a living intelligence that is behind life itself. By adopting these principles we can align ourself with this intelligence and start to bring about the change that many feel is so badly needed.

The planet that we have lived upon has managed itself for billions of years, maintaining a balance whereby the life that it sustained did not draw out more than it put in. Life has been perfectly recycled at every level without any accumulation of toxic waste or any diminishing of the natural resources that support it. The oceans and rivers remained pure and teemed with life, the oxygen cycle and the nitrogen cycle were kept perfectly in balance, and nothing that died failed to decay without leaving any toxic residue from its presence here. And all of this without anyone managing it or interfering with it in any way.

As humanity we have, over the last few hundred years, continuously taken out more than we put in to the pool of resource that we rely upon. We have accumulated, as a result, vast quantities of toxic waste that will take thousands of years to degrade. In doing so, we have broken the balance and cycles of life that we actually depend upon. Our soils, oceans, forests and rivers have been depleted more in the past ten years than in the twenty before that, more in the last thirty than the hundred before that, more in the last hundred years than in the whole of the history of our planet before that point.[3]

---

3   Hard data from WWF's annual Living Planet report demonstrates this demise. Starting around 1970 we crossed an invisible boundary when the planet no longer replenished its resources faster than humans consumed them. We began to take more from the planet each year than it could restore. The processes of regeneration – such as plants regrowing, fish stocks rebuilding and carbon being re-absorbed from the air – are being depleted and destroyed. For the last fifty years, the gap between our rate of consumption and the planet's rate of regeneration has widened. Earth Overshoot Day is the moment each year when humankind's use of natural resources exceeds the planet's ability to produce and replenish them. The first Earth Overshoot Day fell in late December 1970. In 2015, it fell on August 13th, in 2016 it fell on August 8th. WWF shows with absolute clarity that Planet Earth is in the red. For the autumn and winter months, people will be writing cheques our planet can't cash. We are spending more than we earn, taking more than is being offered. This is a clear example of society taking out more than we put in. Debating this is not the purpose of this book but I think most people will agree this is the case.

The question is, can we reverse the trend? Rather than assume we can continue to take out whatever we want regardless of cost, can we start to explore how we might give something back so the planet has the space to breathe out once again? At an individual level, can we change our consumption patterns so that we are taking out only our fair share of what the planet can replenish? It's a tough and inconvenient question to be asking. The answer right now is probably no. But this book is not an environmental and ecological call to action. I am simply asking these questions as a basis from which to start our investigation; our investigation into how life reached this point and what would be the grounds for deep change to come about joyfully, rather than reluctantly within each of us individually.

We have gradually lost sight of that first basic principle of life: that if we expect or even hope to flourish in the future we should not expect to take out more than we put in. In our shift towards an ever more materialist view of life, we have come to value life in terms of the things we are able to acquire, rather than the quality of the experience we are having. As a result, we have experienced the suffering that is caused by failing to live in accordance with the intelligence behind our lives.

In the early morning I meditate. Early, when the world is still sleeping and at rest. And in the stillness, I tune in to the energy of everything that is going on around us endlessly. And there are two things that I feel remain when my mind has stopped. The first is the sublimely peaceful, harmonious, even blissful rhythm of life as an expression of the natural order. Life! Coming into being, growing and passing away as it has done for billions of years. There is the subtlest rhythm to it, and not the slightest feeling of tension or friction. Always and everywhere it rests effortlessly within itself. There is such a profound feeling of love behind it all, in spite of the hardships and struggles that are sometimes involved in coming to life and passing away.

And then I feel the energy of man. The energy of the will of man and the mass of humanity upon this earth. And I feel the unbearable tension that humanity is living in, in its effort to hold sway over its domain and bend it to its will. I feel the impact of this upon the natural order and the creaking and straining that it produces.

As I sit with these two inexorable energies, I tune into the stillness from which all of it is arising and I know that there is never a hair out of place. The world and the universe always and everywhere expresses itself the only way it ever could. For billions of years this planet expressed itself perfectly. It was just a shame that no one was here to witness its extraordinarily beautiful display.

Well now we are here, and we can witness it. It is easy to come to the end of a life having toiled to uphold our personal world. Bemoaning the loss of it as it is stripped from us with our final breath, it would be easy to have been here without ever stopping to take stock of what we have been a part of. That would be the greatest tragedy imaginable.

There is little doubt that if we all departed in a

puff of smoke right now, the planet would breathe a huge sigh of relief and within a hundred years or so it would be the majestic, sublimely imaginative and creative display that it always has been. It would be such a shame if once again no one was here to witness it in the way we as humans have a capacity to do. So the question really is not whether we survive, but the quality of life we are going to create in our efforts to survive. The purpose of this book is to investigate this question as honestly and realistically as we can, and in doing so, to seek solutions that will point a way to a wholly positive and life enriching future not just for us as humans, but for all beings who are sharing in the extraordinary experience of being alive.

* * *

Key Survival Point For Staying Conscious

Learn not to ignore things but to look as honestly as you can at life and what is going on around you. Try to stand courageously in the face of whatever you see rather than pretend it is not happening.

(You might like to listen to the accompanying album Brave Souls, Track 2. What Lies In The Stillness)

2

A Momentum For
Positive Change

Best-selling author and New York Times journalist *Chris Hedges*, in his brutally honest book *The World As It Is*, quite simply says:

"Our way of life is over. Our profligate consumption is finished. Our children will never have the standard of living we had."

When we look into the challenges before us, the tendency is to assume that it is an economic or an environmental crisis that we face. I am suggesting that it may be a spiritual and moral crisis as well, and that if we can address this, our chances of resolving our other challenges are hugely increased.

At almost every level of our lives there are clear indications that we might have to embrace a wholesale change in the way we approach life. The signs are not hard to see for any of us who are prepared to pay attention. And yet, so far, we have either been unable or unwilling to find the determination required to seek the solutions that are being asked or demanded of us. The solutions that will ensure our well-being in the here and now and the well-being of those who will follow in our footsteps.

The more time I spend in the UK, the more I sense that people are increasingly numb and disconnected. I can feel this numbness creeping up on all of us, myself included. And it is often hard to spot it happening.

By numb, I mean we are losing our capacity to feel deeply and meet our experiences with full awareness. In short we are becoming desensitised, and the result is that we become increasingly willing to accept things in our lives, and in the world around us, that we would find unacceptable if we were not numb. This cuts deep, and it is profoundly upsetting. While we are more connected than ever before through technology and social media, it has encouraged us to become intoxicated with ourselves and for many has exacerbated a need to be seen. We have become so distracted by it all that we are losing touch with that place in the heart where we're all connected and what it is that we are connected to.

I am always being asked for advice on how people can improve their feeling of contentment and personal meaning. I can honestly say that in fifteen years I can count on one hand the number of people for whom the answer to this question isn't just "simplify your life and get rid of what you don't need (preferably by giving it to someone who does)". The Buddha used to say that "One who is of few needs and easy to serve is close to being happy; one who is of many needs and hard to serve is far from being happy".

It seems so clear the world so needs each of us to start giving back. Every day that we take out more than we put in, our soul withers in some small way.

Every day we put in more than we take out, our souls shine a little more brightly. Perhaps it is time to stop asking what's in it for me, and start asking what have I got to give?

We are all intelligent enough to see what is happening to us if we are willing to pay attention honestly. But our welfare in the future will not be built on understanding alone, it will be built on conduct and choices. We are living, both individually and globally, the effect of our past choices. Our life will roll out in the future as a reflection of the choices we make now. This is now, as it has always been, the predicament and challenge that faces mankind, each of us as individuals, together as groups and as a species seeking to secure our long term future, survival and happiness upon this earth.

A cluttered and overcomplicated life leaves little room for contentedness, happiness and inner peace. The more we have around us, the more vexing it is to maintain. At every level, simplification and a lighter footprint is the way forward. We all need to step back and catch our breath. By working, sharing and collaborating together, whilst learning to be of few needs and easy to serve, we can change our world dramatically for the better.

There is a lot of positive movement in many quarters to seek out solutions to our problems, but all too often such initiatives are occurring on the fringes of society. It is all too easy to reflect upon the challenges we face and feel they constitute an insurmountable problem. This is why we have to start at home, with ourselves, by simply asking, "How can I respond to what is happening to us?" It is not enough to wait for change to be initiated from the top down. We must remember the 100th monkey effect, where behavioural change is initiated one person at a time, until a point comes where enough critical mass is achieved to prompt widespread change to be adopted across the entire population. Be the change, set an example and let it spread organically.

The real movement towards change is going to be a folk movement. The real revolution is going to have to start in our own hearts and minds as we look deeply at how we have reached the point that we have and imaginatively seek solutions. I don't believe there is a macro solution to be found. Rather than waiting to see what our leaders are going to do and which way our economy is going to go, our first step is to make a personal resolution to place our longing for peace and happiness at the head of our agenda and to stop being a burden to the world. This can become our own individual responsibility, should we choose. Once we decide to take responsibility into our own hands, the feeling of helplessness is transformed into faith and courage. From there solutions will present themselves, but they won't if we just sit back and wait to see how it all pans out. That's indolence, and indolence in many ways is the most insipid of all weaknesses, for it would allow us not to act even when the way ahead is blatantly obvious. If ever there was a time to dig deep and find courage, it is now.

For the past fifteen years I have been teaching meditation to groups of predominantly fortunate individuals. The only way I justify teaching such a group instead of seeking, in some way, to be of service to those whose needs are truly great, is because I live in the hope and belief that each of us, if we choose, could make the decision to stop being a burden in our time here and genuinely seek ways in which we can bring benefit to the world that we are a part of.

Everyone is interested in their welfare, but somehow we have lost sight of where our real welfare lies and what it truly stands upon. It doesn't stand upon our capacity to bend things to our will. It stands only upon our learning to live in alignment with the greater intelligence behind life.

In the past the path out of suffering was traditionally one of renunciation. Yet I believe in the current age there is another path. For the vast majority of us I see a route out of suffering that is not to don robes but to dedicate a proportion of our time, energy and resources to the service and benefit of others and our planet as a whole.

For those of you who are inspired to change, who are feeling the call to a new way of life, my one piece of advice is that time is of the essence. Do not delay. Go out with conviction and exigency and find out what you have to give. Do it now, while the fire in your belly is still strong. Don't let's get to the end of our lives wishing we had done more to find out what it was really all about. There can be no greater calling than to live this precious human existence well and seek ways to become the source of true happiness, both for ourselves and others.

If ever there was a time to stand tall it is now. A time like this won't come around again. We may never again be called upon to find greatness within our hearts. Let us not sleep now when it is time to act. Let us go out there and see what we have to give, so that even if we do not succeed in our efforts, we will do so doing greatly, and never stand amongst those timid souls who know not victory nor defeat.

* * *

Key Survival Point For Staying Conscious

Explore the idea that we are not just facing an environmental and economic crisis, but a spiritual and moral one. Until our basic attitudes to life and what it means to be a human change, we are unlikely to find solutions to the worldly challenges facing us.

3

Reconnecting To
What Really Matters

The aspirations and the hopes and dreams that well up within the hearts of all of us individually are the most profound things that ever happen to us in our life. The calling, the longing for happiness, the longing for peace, the longing to understand and find meaning in our lives call to us all somewhere inside, and when we fail to acknowledge that call, a part of us dries up and becomes numb.

So finding our own relationship with these really big threads in our lives is a very personal thing, and it is a very moving thing. A lot of our inner conflict, even our suffering, is born of the fact that we know that there's something calling in our heart that isn't being expressed or honoured. Feeling disconnected from what is sacred to us is one of the greatest causes of suffering of all. Feeling, honouring and nurturing that connection gives us an inner strength that makes most of the hardships that we do encounter manageable.

So the getting in touch with our heart, listening to it and responding to it, or at least feeling that we are moving in that direction, is one of the things that lifts the weight off us. It makes us feel encouraged and enthusiastic about life. When we lose that connection, we feel we lose a part of ourself.

At a soul level, each one of us is still looking to get in touch with something we feel is there, or know we have experienced at times in our lives, even if we cannot fully grasp exactly what it is. Whether it comes to us in a quiet moment alone in nature when we are moved by its beauty, or when we dance together in celebration of what it is to be alive, somewhere we know it as a connection we long for deeply. It's that getting in touch that I think brings our whole journey in this life alive at a profoundly moving, meaningful level, that suddenly takes the weight off all the other stuff we thought we were here to do.

We are today more virtually connected to each other than we have ever been before, and yet more people than ever before are feeling a quiet state of despair and disconnection in their lives. Whilst we have found numerous ways to comfort ourselves and make our lives more convenient, degenerative sickness such as stress, anxiety, depression and auto-immune diseases are on the increase.

According to psychologist Martin Seligman, major depression is the number one psychological disorder in the western world. One in four people in the UK are likely to experience mental health disorders.[4] In the last 10 years there has been a 68% increase in mental disorders in young people age 5-16. It is now believed that major depression will be the second most disabling condition in the world by 2020 behind heart disease. Ten times more people suffer

4   www.mind.org.uk

from major depression now than in 1945, immediately after the war.

There has never been so much good fortune in the world but this good fortune has failed to translate into a reduction in suffering. The things that once appeared as the sign of good fortune are in the process of becoming the very opposite. The technological advances that added convenience to our lives, many people now feel are close to overwhelming us, and as a result we are witnessing fundamental changes in the way we function at a human level.

Perhaps it is time for us to take stock of the effect that the quest for endless progress is having upon the quality of our lives and the qualities of our minds at a deeper level. Although we have managed to create a convenient life for ourselves, the jury is out as to whether we are finding that life to be more meaningful, enriching or fulfilling.

The way we behave, how we connect to each other, and how we think and process our experience is changing us in ways that we may not yet fully understand, and it is happening quickly. If we don't take stock of the situation we may find it will have overwhelmed us before we know it. And then, somewhere, sometime down the line, we will all come out of the shock of it, and gasping for breath we will start to ask ourselves – "What on earth just happened?"

How often do we stop to reflect upon how rare and fortunate a human life such as this actually is? I think it is quite a common thread in the West, especially amongst those with great fortune, that we develop a sense of entitlement towards life. It is all too easy to feel that we are entitled to having our way, so that when we don't get it we feel disappointed, let down or even angry and resentful. And that sense of entitlement is very difficult to free ourselves from. Often the last thing we might think to do is to find the inner courage and the resolve to embrace our challenges and see if they might carry some lessons for us to learn from. Ultimately it is up to us whether we allow our challenges to be our undoing or our invitation to evolve.

What we perceive our needs to be are often not our needs but our wants. Our needs are really far less than we might imagine. There are the basic requisites for the supporting of a human life, so that it is not just a struggle for survival from start to finish. For those of us fortunate enough to have good health, sound mind, food, shelter and companionship, our life is an opportunity to explore what it is to be human, and beyond that to see what we might do to make this world a better place.

The Buddha cast his mind out all that time ago upon the world and made the reflection: "Truly as humans we get ourselves entangled in the most tangled knot of suffering". He saw how we have the potential to bring ourselves to so much suffering through not understanding the implications of the choices we make. The Buddha was so vexed by this tendency to turn our rare good fortune as humans into unnecessary suffering that he gave up his life of privilege as a Prince and went forth in search of a way to break the cycle of suffering.

In the years that followed he trained his mind through the practice of meditation and so matured his capacity to pay attention to what is actually unfolding behind the process of life. He came to understand not only the nature of suffering and its causes, but the conditions by which such suffering comes to an end. What he saw was that when we live in alignment with the innate intelligence of life itself, beings flourish and prosper. But when they live in conflict, they come to no end of suffering.

When we look for ourselves, it is plain to see that for all the physical hardship that exists in this world, there are countless unfortunate folk who, although challenged, meet their challenges daily and find grace within their lives. Equally there are countless fortunate folk who, blessed with the most extraordinary good fortune, are still deeply miserable and dissatisfied. Clearly it is not so much what we experience in life that determines our happiness or lack of it, but the quality of mind with which we meet these experiences.

Right now each and every day we are living, individually, communally, culturally, and globally, the effect of our past choices. Our life will roll out in the future as a reflection of the choices we make now. The choices we make as individuals, together as groups, and as a species, will determine our long term future, survival and happiness upon this earth. We are a resourceful species and when it comes to finding ways to survive, there are no ends of means at our disposal.

Happiness, on the other hand, is harder won. Our survival in no way guarantees our happiness. It takes tremendous care, generosity of spirit and self-honesty to secure a happy, meaningful and rewarding passage in our time upon this earth. Though precious indeed this human life is not easy to navigate skilfully, and to come to the end of it knowing that it was a well lived and enjoyed, deeply enriching experience is something that takes real integrity, intelligence and consciousness.

This is our life, and to each one of us it is precious indeed. It is important to all of us to be happy and at peace with who we are and the world around us. In truth, there is nothing we long for more.

* * *

Key Survival Point For Staying Conscious

When we disconnect from our heart and its real aspirations, hopes and dreams, we are often left with a feeling that life lacks meaning and is empty. This is one of the reasons we end up pursuing our desires in the hope that they will give us the sense of meaning we have lost. Ask yourself from your heart, "What do I really want out of life?" The answer may not be what you initially would think.

4

Does Flourishing Mean We
Always Need More?

So, as an exercise, following on from what we were discussing in the previous chapter, let's take a brief look at our lives and see what is going on. Normally we might be inclined to judge the success of our lives in terms of whether things are going our way or not. And certainly none of us wants to feel that life is an endless uphill struggle. But here I want to look at how we are faring within ourselves in our efforts to progress with whatever we are doing with our lives. So for this I want to identify three states of being that we might find ourselves in from time to time. These I will call, struggling, coping and flourishing.

So, firstly the state of struggling. This is when life is a real battle simply to stay on top of things, or where we may even feel overwhelmed. In the struggling state, there is little respite and we constantly have to manage ourselves and juggle things just to keep our heads above water.

Our life can all too easily become a struggle without us realising it's a struggle. We feel that we're not quite on top of everything. We feel, "If I was to just let go or relax even just a little bit it would all fall apart". Well, if our life would fall apart on account of us not being in control of it all the time, then this might suggest that our life is organised in an unmanageable way. This often happens when our desires outstrip our capacity and the desires are neither in alignment with the energy that is actually supporting our lives or the energy that we actually have.

In both of these scenarios the effort and energy required to get what we want is so demanding that even if we do succeed we are so exhausted that we are unable to enjoy either the journey or the fruits of our endeavour. Perhaps we could investigate this and look at what is actually driving us, and see whether there really is supportive energy for it. Life should not be something that we have to desperately struggle to hold together. It may be worth considering, if we are struggling, that this is a sign that the life we have created for ourselves is in conflict with the energy that is actually supporting it.

So we can find ourselves in a state of struggle for sustained periods, and it's not uncommon that we would struggle through our entire life. What's more, it may never occur to us to allow our lives to fundamentally reorganise into a state where we are coping better. Often all it takes for us to move out of a state where we are struggling is to simply let go of some of the things we are struggling to hold together or to just realign ourselves more realistically. But sadly, even more often what happens is that things stay stuck in such a state until they fall apart. Either we do, or our world around us falls to pieces. However, if things do fall apart, even though we may consider it to be a failure, somewhere inside, if we can get over our pride, there comes a feeling of relief that we don't have to struggle like that any more. Many people report feeling a strange sense of relief on being told they are chronically ill because it means they no longer have to struggle to hold their lives together.

The next state is the one that most of us exist in, which is just coping. In the coping state we might feel that "I still have to make quite an effort to stay on top of things but I'm OK, I'm muddling through". This coping state is the borderline between having access to all of our potential and actually using most of our energy to stay on top of our life.

In this state there's not much left over by the time we've attended to what needs to be attended to. This is coping. What we're taking out of life and what it costs us energetically or at every other level to maintain it, these factors are only just about in balance and so there's not much in reserve.

One of the problems is that because we are always asking ourselves, "How can I take the most out of life?", every step of the way, we tend to incline ourselves to this state where the best that we can do is cope. Why does this occur so often? Possibly it is because at every opportunity we have to take more out of life, we do take more out. And of course the taking more out requires that we have to put more into it. This can happen at every level, energetically, emotionally, physically, financially and materially. As soon as we get a little bit more money we'll go and spend it, or as soon as we can borrow more money we'll borrow it. We live our life in this constant state where it's OK, but if things significantly change it could all come tumbling down. This is just getting by or coping. Things aren't going wrong but we don't have much room to relax or breathe. We are working at the limit of our capacity with not much left in reserve. We might be getting done everything that is asked of us, but we have little time or energy left to enjoy or appreciate our efforts.

This seems to be our innate tendency, this desire to always seek to take out more. And every step of the way in the taking out more, we demand more of ourselves. So we tie ourselves up in this state where, in our efforts to keep adding more to our lives, the only way we can do this is by just muddling through - by just coping.

The third state is a state I call flourishing. This is where your life stands upon a deeply embodied energetic support that upholds it - that you can rest upon, that you can reply upon, you feel comfortable in the knowledge that it is there, in the background, and that your life is not an act of personal will but a reflection of the life force and energy that is flowing through it. You are not constantly grappling to hold it together, it's an expression of the conditions that are working through your life in support of it. And so you can rest upon that supportive energy, and flow with it.

In that situation we find that it doesn't take all of our energy to hold our life together. We now have the opportunity to apply what energy we have to the expression of life itself, to see how completely we can embody that life that is moving through us, and to express it or experience it. This is the point that we start to feel really alive and connected to life.

So I think it is constructive to honestly look at these three states and take a snapshot of our own life. When we do look honestly we can see that life is full of choices and that what we choose defines our life. It is in truth so wonderfully simple and so clearly the case. The skill lies in making wise choices.

Over the years of teaching meditation and helping people on retreat I have seen in so many cases very fortunate people who are struggling and yet really don't need to be. What's more, almost everybody who's coping could, if they reorganise their life, be flourishing. Yet it's a rare handful of people who truly flourish in the expression of their life so that they rest in a deeply settled way upon it, so that it's a very enriching, fulfilling and satisfying experience through and through. Such people are usually an inspiration to others but they are rare it seems.

This is a shame, because once we truly do get to that place when we really know that we have got more than we need, the next thing that arises in our mind is a tremendous sense of gratitude and the desire to give something back, or to share it.

What if we could all reorganise ourselves in such a way, that those of us who are struggling looked at why, addressed it, and at least got to the state where we could cope? And those of us who were coping looked at why we're only coping and perhaps asked ourselves, "If I was to take less out, maybe my life would be more manageable and I'd might actually find that I have far more to give?"

At that point we'll be able to look back to those who are struggling and reflect that with a little bit of help, I dare say that they could cope better or even get to the place where they might flourish. When we stop always asking, "What more could I possibly get out of this life and the world around me?" we start to recognise what we might be able to put into the pot, give back, and offer up.

Resolving the unsustainable muddle that we are getting ourselves into as a modern society could possibly be that simple. It's not about looking at the great big picture and wondering how on earth this tangled knot of humanity is going to sort its stuff out. It might just take a simple act of generosity from each of us with the decision to take out less and learn to appreciate and make more of what we have.

The muddle that we find ourselves in is only a reflection of what I have just described to you: the tendency to assume and the feeling that we always need more to make us happy. And so all too often, not only do we end up consuming far more than we really need to, we get ourselves locked into a state where we struggle endlessly, or merely cope, but rarely end up flourishing, when we could be having the most amazing time here.

I think it is important that we get out of our heads the idea that flourishing means having, taking, gaining, winning or earning more. I've worked with some of the most fortunate people on this planet, in positions of extraordinary prestige and respect and authority, such that society would probably admire them, and do you know what? Most of them are in every bit as much of a muddle as the ordinary folk, and often far more.

When I look, I just don't see a correlation between how much one takes out of life and how happy one ends up being. I really, really don't. I've looked honestly and deeply and there isn't a correlation that I have found. Of course not having the basic requirement to support a life is another thing, and there are countless poor souls alive right now who genuinely are struggling to stay alive. But for those of us who are blessed with such rare and extraordinary good fortune, to be making such heavy weather of our efforts to find happiness is a great shame. And even more so when we look at what it costs to keep us here in our less than satisfied state.

The balance between what we take out and what we put back I truly believe is the axis, the tipping point. It is the turning point where life and everything in it all starts to reorganise itself into an infinitely more balanced and coherent state. When we start to reapply that energy we have expended in our efforts to 'take out', towards the investigation of, "How can I put more into this?" everything gets transformed profoundly.

Surely this makes sense, doesn't it? We still might end up looking out at the world and practically go, "No, I can't see that ever happening", but I would implore you not to be defeatist! Because it only needs us, any one of us, one person at a time, to see how far we could ride with that, so that the next person sees what's happened to us - that our anxiety has gone, our fear and worry about where it all leads has gone. And why has it all gone? Because we've surrendered to that process of giving to life, and trusted it. Life itself is a creative process. It is infinitely giving by nature. When we become like that ourselves we really reconnect to what it is to be alive.

Each one of us who starts to turn around our lives might just touch the next person and prompt them to think, "Hold on, maybe there's something in this." So let's not wait for the next person to change, they may never, and it doesn't matter. The world takes its time working its stuff out. But when it occurs to you to change, and in that moment that it occurs to you, you realise there was a moment of clarity, not confusion, then you should stand upon that, and you should act upon that.

When seeking a resolution to a challenge or problem we should always stand upon the conclusions we come to when our minds are balanced and clear, and reject the conclusions we come to when we are smothered with confusion, worry or fear. We all know deep down, somewhere inside, that a life as fortunate as this is an opportunity to put something back into the pot, and we all know, somewhere inside, when we find our own special way of doing that we'll feel in some way more complete.

When we feel the balance in our life between what we're taking out and what we are giving, we feel that inside, and the ease and the absence of friction that brings will be enough to tell us that's the way to go. In truth we never feel as satisfied in the acquisition of our desires as we do when we have given of ourselves in some way that we feel is meaningful. We are creaking, and our world is creaking, from the energy it has taken to try to find ever new and novel ways to take more out of the system. It really is the case that the answer to so many of our problems, personal, social, economic and environmental, lies in the simple decision to start giving back. It couldn't actually be more simple than that.

* * *

Key Survival Point For Staying Conscious

Is it really enough to just cope? Ask yourself, "How much of my life has been a struggle? How much of my life have I spent just coping? How much of my life have I felt that I am actually flourishing?"

Reflect upon how this might change if you simplified your life. Instead of trying to put as many things as you can into it, try to bring more quality to the things that you do.

5

Are We As Conscious
As We Think We Are?

"We think too much and feel too little."
                              - Charlie Chaplin

Have you noticed how when you ask someone how they feel, what they will almost always tell you is what they're thinking? When asked, "How do you feel?", instinctively we go up to our mind to ask ourself how we feel, because we don't know how we feel!

How and what we feel is the deepest and most direct connection there is to the experience we are actually having. We spend so much of our early days at school being taught how to think, but very little guidance is given to help us develop our ability to feel. These days our minds tend to run on full throttle from the moment we wake to the moment we fall asleep. Habitually we tend to live with little stillness within the mind. With all the noise it makes and all the attention it gets we may be losing our ability to connect to and to feel what we are experiencing at a deeper level. Once we start to lose this directly felt connection to our experience, we are left only with our ideas and thoughts about what is going on. In the absence of that deeper sense of connectedness, we create ideas and tell ourselves stories to compensate for the sense that there is something lacking. But this sense of lacking in truth is a by-product of our inability to pay sufficient attention to what is happening and what we are doing to find the magic in it. Charlie Chaplin summed this tendency up perfectly: "We think too much, we feel too little".

I read in the paper the other day that some children now have to be taught what certain facial expressions mean because they are not developing their ability to feel or to empathise. This is about the most alarming thing that could be happening to us, because the one thing that marks us as different from most other forms of life is that very ability to perceive the depth and felt texture of our experience directly at a level beyond concrete thought alone. It is that ability to feel deeply what is happening to us that makes us truly human.

Being alive is a deeply felt experience, it is not just a mental exercise, and the loss of that feeling, tone or texture to our experience is what causes us to retreat up into our head and start to live a cerebral version, or if you like our own virtual version of reality. We end up living our own inner version of 'life according to me' instead of just living life as it is.

In doing so we end up with an increasing sense of separation, if not isolation, from the actual experience we are having and we lose the connection between what is going on within us and what is going on around us. It is feeling connected to what we are experiencing that makes it feel meaningful and alive. When we stop feeling life, a disconnect occurs and so instead we end up lost in thinking and inevitably come to the conclusion that life is a lonely and isolated place. We end up all living our own virtual inner versions of reality and there is no one who is actually sharing in that experience but us. In effect we are alone, in our inner world. And in that aloneness we start to shut down our ability to connect in a number of ways. It is a self-perpetuating process, a catch-22 if you like. We perceive that we don't like what we feel so we shut down, but the feeling we find most difficult to be with is the very feeling of being shut down itself, and the bland, numb sense of lacking that comes upon us in its absence.

The funny thing about being numb is that we don't know we're numb, because that's the nature of numbness; we can't feel it, can we?! If we could feel it, we wouldn't be numb. So we don't know where to look when we start to unpackage the things that might be holding us back or limiting us. We can't see. We can sit down and try and make sense of it but if we are numb we can't feel we are numb.

So the journey home, or back to our root, if you like, is actually an exercise in being with ourselves as we are, warts and all. It is about being yourself and experiencing how you really feel, until you can be with it enough that something deeper starts to come through and something inside you shifts. Whatever it is that unlocks us individually so that we are willing to really start feeling again or to start using our actual experience as our reference rather than our ideas of what is happening is a very personal thing.

Our deeper capacity to feel can be shut down by a number of things. It can be caused by:

- the way we live our lives
- how we deal with what happens to us
- the ambient environment we are living in

All of these produce stress and dysfunction in the body's subtle energetic mechanisms through which we do actually feel. We will look at how this happens in more detail in the coming chapters.

Often these days we tend to replace the feeling that might be associated with the experiences we have with the ideas we create about them. We don't connect through the actual experience we are sharing but through the ideas we formulate about that experience. The Buddha called this being 'view-rooted' as opposed to 'experience-rooted'. What he meant was that some of us refer more to our ideas about the experience in order to make it appear valid than we do to the actual experience itself.

The problems that arise from being too 'view-rooted' are many. The most moving aspects of life are deeply felt experiences and not ideas: love, grief, gratitude, appreciation, joy, wonder, awe. Our ideas are in truth just a figment of our imagination. We can dream up almost any kind of take on almost every experience we have. But ideas are not the experience itself, they are our take on the experience. Feeling arises much more immediately within the experience itself than do our ideas. The problem is that we spend so much time thinking about things that we often miss the main event as it happens.

I was walking with one of my students just before lunch yesterday and he found this squirrel lying beside the drive. Its back was broken and we picked it up and we sat with it for a while, trying to figure out what to do with this poor little thing. It wasn't dead, I couldn't work out how close to death it was and so what to do? And so I thought, well, there's part of this poor animal that is going to be in shock by being held by these brutes that it spends its entire life running away from. And another part of me is feeling to give it as much love and care as I possibly could. And as I looked deeply at it, it wasn't obviously suffering. It actually looked at peace. It was so surrendered to what was happening; there was something so graceful about it in its suffering.

We held it and then we thought, well, let's leave it somewhere peaceful so that if it dies, it dies in its own environment, unvexed by anything except the passing away process. And we left it there in the long grass in the shade of a tree and I sent love to it as we meditated later. As I did I thought to myself, "Oh no, dying alone. The poor thing. Have I done the right thing?" So I went and told Sati who was cooking in the kitchen and she said, "Oh no! where is it? where is it?" So we went and we brought it in and she picked it up and she held it in her hands, looking down at this dear creature in its plight.

This whole experience with the squirrel was not something going on in our heads, in the same way that our connection to this experience of life that we are all sharing is not something going on in our heads. It is much deeper and more immediate than that. There it was, the life of this little thing, the only life it had, in peril and it was going to die. There was nothing we could do to help it but be with it. I thought, "Just be with this little thing." Sati held it, and she went to get warm milk, and tried to feed it warm milk on the tip of her finger. And then at one point its little hand grabbed her finger, and it opened its eyes one last time...and there was something in its eyes, it was saying, "I see you, I'm there with you. You are here with me." And as it opened its eyes and passed away there was such an overwhelming feeling that it had been met.

Now how can you explain that? You can't explain it, but you can feel it. These things go on at the level at which we actually connect, when we know we're sharing an experience and we feel it deeply, even though we haven't figured it out in our minds. This is our ability to be fully in and with our experience, and this is something that goes on at the heart level. It is when we start to lose that ability to connect and to feel that we start to lose the essence of what it is to be human. We need to reflect, what might it mean to lose that deep connection to life? As that little animal died in her arms, of course she felt bereft, stroking it, crying; "Oh no, don't die, please don't die." She sat with it for fifteen minutes hoping that it would open up its little eyes again...and I could feel her pain. Who would want to lose the ability to feel that? Yet we all too easily do.

There are two ways that we lose our capacity to feel. One is by shutting down, and the other is through atrophy; we just stop using that capacity. When things happen to us in life that we struggle to accept as the truth, the subtle part of our software system in the heart that actually allows us to feel deeply shrinks, retracts or shuts down in some way. This is how many of us deal with challenging experiences like grief, loss, disappointment or extreme stress: we shut off the experience. At an energetic level, that is what ignorance is: the part of us that feels the unpleasant experience shuts down so that we no longer feel it. And in doing so we become emotionally numb. A typical example of this process at work can be seen in the way that many of us deal with disappointment in relationships. If we feel let down by one person it often prompts us to shut down a part of our heart that leaves us unable to open to others in the future. It seems that sometimes to have little feeling for someone is our only protection against feeling too much.

When we experience something that we personally feel unable to accept, it causes shrinking, a shielding, or a shutting down at a subtle energetic level, that reduces the current of life moving through us. This allows us to feel less intensely should the same thing happen to us again in the future. The problem with shutting down our capacity to feel the unpleasant is that we use the same mechanism to feel the pleasant. When we refuse to acknowledge our pain we diminish our capacity to feel joy.

I remember when I was a kid the profound experience of seeing someone shot dead in an old Western movie. Not only did it bring home the sure truth that death is a part of life and it could happen at any time, but in that moment I felt the intense feeling of loss, as I realised that even though the one shot was a baddy, he was losing his life, and that is something so very precious to him. The feeling was strong and moving and powerful, and it worked upon me at a level far beyond my understanding.

These days we are capable of witnessing no end of horror, in movies, in the media, all around us. And we are able to do so because we don't feel anything like as much as we used to. We are losing our capacity to empathise. This may well be the only protection we have against feeling too much, in a world where we constantly stimulate and bombard our senses in ways that just a generation ago would have been considered inhumane and probably unbearable. But now in this world it seems like the only thing we can do. The problem with this, of course, is that if we stop feeling pain we likewise stop feeling joy. The mechanism by which we feel these things is the same.

Just as an exercise, let me ask you to cast your mind back 15 years or so - if you are older go back 20 or 25 years. Spend a few minutes remembering how you used to feel. See if you can remember a time where you were deeply moved by a beautiful piece of music, or a song, or a painting or a view of nature in its splendour, or the innocence of a puppy, or the joy of a child at play, or your own joy as a child at play. Now ask yourself:

- "Do I feel these things more deeply or less deeply today than I used to?"
- "Do I think more about everything these days than I used to?"

Learning to feel deeply again is a very moving experience, and it takes self-honesty and acceptance to do it. It puts us in touch with everything that hurts, it puts us in touch with everything that's been painful, but it also puts us in touch with all of our deeper feelings of joy, love, compassion, enthusiasm, gratitude and appreciation. Making the decision to learn to feel deeply again also involves choices.

It involves making choices about whether or not we are going to honour this life of ours, the essence of it, and get back in touch with it, or continue to pursue our desires or wants and run from our aversions, regardless of what that might be doing to us at a deeper level. One of the functions of our nerve system is that it regulates the degree to which it is sensitised depending upon how stimulated it is. The more stimulated we become, the more it has to shut down its capacity to feel so that we are not overwhelmed by it.

When I watched that Western when I was eight years old my operating system was wide open, and my capacity to feel what was going on within me and around me was very subtle. There is no way that that operating system could possibly have dealt with a modern action movie, let alone the sheer pace and level of stimulation we experience in today's modern world. But whilst we may have been more sensitive than we are today, we were also more subtle in our capacity to feel deeply what was going on within and around us. And as such we were able to find joy in simpler things and so were far more easily satisfied then, than we are today.

I remember one Christmas when I was eight, coming downstairs before anyone had woken to see if Santa had taken his brandy and orange from the mantelpiece. As I walked into the sitting room, I couldn't believe my eyes. There, fully laid out across the room, was a Lego train set, with an engine that actually ran on a battery powered motor. As I explored it in awe, in the silence of that early Christmas morning, I felt the love of my parents as they sat up late the night before, piecing their gift for me together. I remember as I sat alone in that room, thinking about all the other kids about to wake up with a sense of wonder and hope, and I felt too those whose dreams would not be met. And in that moment of deep joy and happiness, I cried to myself. I had no idea why I was doing it, it came up from a place inside me, and I never once stopped to think about what was happening. I simply felt in all its depth the entirety of the moment I was in.

When desires proliferate they become craving and addiction. When this happens the enthusiasm that comes with our desires is eroded. At one level we've got more desire today that we have ever had, but it is not at all clear that much enthusiasm now accompanies that desire. The danger then is that we lose any sense of satisfaction when our desires are actually met. In many ways the increase in the feeling of wanting and desiring things is a reflection of the fact that we are no longer satisfied with the things we already have. It seems as if almost nothing satisfies us any more. Our food needs to be sweeter and stronger tasting, our music louder, our drugs stronger, our sex more imaginative or excessive. As our ability to feel has gradually shut down, it takes more and more to satisfy us. Again, another catch-22.

In the West we often hear it said that we are the most fortunate beings on the planet. Are we sure that is still the case? I remember while walking in Burma some years ago passing through a village in which five kids were playing cricket on an ox track, with a tree stump, a broom handle and a punctured and threadbare tennis ball. I sat and watched them for an hour or so as they screamed with joy, hugged and jostled with each other. Their eyes shone like diamonds, and on their faces was nothing but the deepest of joy. As I sat in their midst I recognised how completely their sense of wonder was still intact.

When I used to live in Bali I built and ran a health detox retreat. It was a programme designed to help people who had become overwhelmed by the stresses of modern life get their health back on track. Over the past fifteen years of teaching meditation and running health retreats I have watched people come for various reasons and many come to put themselves back together again because at some level they feel broken. Well, fifteen years ago when we sent out the booking form, asking for people's dietary requirements, we might get one or two people who might be gluten, wheat or dairy intolerant or whatever. Now it's not unusual for as many as half the people coming to have complex dietary requirements.

Have we understood what intolerance actually is? It's exactly that – intolerance. I am not talking about allergies; an allergy is a different thing and much harder to address, although effectively it is an extreme intolerance to something. Yes of course, part of the problem is that our digestive system is out of balance, usually because of the poor nature of the nutrition, but a large part of intolerance is produced by the mind. When the mind becomes intolerant towards inconvenience or challenges, a subtle mechanism of the mind by which we integrate our experiences becomes unstable. At this point the mind becomes excessively reactive and this hyper-reactivity translates into intolerances at both a mental and physiological level. Literally we overreact to the things that we are exposed to. This increase in intolerance accounts for the stress that people go through when they can't get their phone charged or the impatience that arises when our internet connection slows down, or we are kept waiting at a checkout counter. I remember when I used to travel around India by train in the early 1990's. Often it was necessary to go the train station a day before the departure to queue for a seat reservation. Whatever has happened to our patience?

So not only are we going through experiences that are grosser and more stimulating than we have ever had before, we are also becoming more and more intolerant. Although we seem quite tolerant of the horror we see in the media, in movies and the violence that is all around us these days, how tolerant are we when someone cuts us up in the traffic on the way to work, let alone if someone criticises our work in some way? The truly alarming thing is that while we may have lost our capacity to feel and empathise, we have actually become less tolerant in our numbness, not more. And why is that? As we have lost our felt connection to others around us, our focus has turned more and more to ourselves. Our idea of ourselves has become so inordinately complex and elaborate in our search for individuality that everything seems to be all about 'me.' We take it all so personally.

So what make us resilient or intolerant? We are either resilient because we are shut down and we don't feel anything, or we are resilient because we are robust and our physical and mental constitution is strong. Although we are exposing ourselves to these extraordinarily stimulating experiences, it's actually not bringing robustness, we're not learning to land them in an integrated way, because they have now become so over-stimulating as to overwhelm us. Although we may not be feeling much consciously we are unconsciously overwhelmed, and it is this being overwhelmed that causes more and more intolerance. We simply cannot be with what is happening to us. Our systems are just not coping with the experiences that we are choosing for ourselves - or maybe not choosing - and so for various reasons our only viable response it to shut down; and so we lose our capacity to feel deeply.

"I need a more exciting time", "I need more of this", "I need to go and do that" – we need more stimulation, more gratification, "more things that might please me because I feel less pleased by what I do". The phone doesn't satisfy us so we get another, the car doesn't satisfy us so we get another, the job doesn't satisfy, we get another, the partner doesn't satisfy, we get another, the hobby doesn't satisfy, we get another. But when life doesn't satisfy, then what...we can't just get another.

At so many levels, how we are living and what

is going on around us is so over-stimulating that the delicate part that adds our sense of meaning, wonder and joy to life is struggling to feel what it used to. We hear so much said about how we have improved the quality of life in our societies in the past fifty years or so, but if that truly was the case, then how do we explain the enormous increase in both physical and mental health problems that people today face, which only fifty years ago were quite rare? Are we really not noticing these things happening? Or do we really think it's OK that they are? So all of these things – whether it's trauma that we have been through, or shock, or continued stress, or over-stimulation, or the degeneration of the nervous system, our life force and internal electrical system - they all cause gradually an atrophy in our resonant life field and with it our capacity to feel.

Our feelings have always been our touchstone that helps us to stay connected to life; to be aware of what is happening to us. Our thoughts and ideas do not perform the same function of maintaining that connection. The more time you spend trying to figure out what life is, the more time you are in the way. What we all need to do is to be able to feel again. When we feel what is happening to us, that feeling becomes our greatest teacher. Because somewhere inside we all have the ability to know what feels right and what doesn't. And this in the end is the intelligence that has the capacity to lead us in the right direction. By shutting ourselves down we allow ourselves to maintain a trajectory that is leading us off course.

That squirrel I talked about earlier, that simple

little life that would otherwise have gone unnoticed in this world, as it passed away it didn't fight with itself. Its little finger came out and wrapped itself around Sati's finger and it opened its eyes and breathed its last breath and it was gone, and it surrendered. It was an extraordinarily moving thing to behold because I really realised, as I had earlier when I was with it and it was struggling and it couldn't move and its back was broken, that its surrender contained no sense of despair, no feeling of, "Oh my goodness what's happening to me? What's going to happen next?" It was just...LIFE...it was a part of it, and as such it wasn't in conflict.

There was so much grace in it. It was just with life, even as it died, it was with its moment. Yes, I know, a lot of us find it hard to surrender when it's time to move on, because it's the idea of ourselves that is being dismantled. But it is only the *idea* of ourselves, that's all. The rest of it is just life passing through us. Life itself is endless. If we are going to create this idea of ourself, it takes courage to acknowledge the fact that it's going to get dismantled one day sooner or later. It wasn't even courage in that little creature as it passed, it was *grace*. It didn't fight, it just was there with it until its last breath. It looked more peaceful through that experience than I've seen any human look for a long time.

So, we do have to ask ourselves whether we are the most conscious beings or whether we are just the ones with the most elaborate ideas about ourselves and what we think life might be. Meanwhile, always and everywhere, out there, beyond the window that protects you from it – everything in nature is resting effortlessly within itself. Life itself is not in conflict. The day the last white rhino or snow leopard is hunted and dies, it will not shed a tear. It will simply mark the end of its time here. It is us who have the capacity to wonder and delight in the miraculous display that life truly is - whose hearts should be breaking. For we will be the ones who are left as witnesses to what remains in the absence of such splendour. Nature itself is the pure expression of the creative intelligence behind all life. Everything in life is busy doing its bit, being its bit of the way of things. None of it is meaningless, all of it is sacred. And in the middle of it all there's us as humans also part of the way of things.

We have this unique capacity to turn up and be aware of what's happening to us at a deeper level than perhaps that squirrel did, but these ideas that we are capable of formulating in our mind have done nothing but separate us from the experience that we are actually having. I have no doubt that many people, including scientists, are going to reject what I am saying for one reason or another. But it doesn't matter. Our ideas are just our ideas. Life is life, and it has never waited for us to figure it out. It goes on everywhere as it always has done.

I would love to suggest that you put this book down right now and head out into the world of nature for long enough to feel again what you are actually a part of...and let that start to talk to you and show you the way! But if you can't do that, then I hope you will read on as we explore what we might do to reconnect to the deepest part of ourselves.

Key Survival Point For Staying Conscious

There is far more to consciousness than intelligence and our ability to think. Feeling is the real essence of our experience. We often use our thinking minds to compensate for the fact that we are numb to the actual experiences we are having. When we learn to feel again (both the pleasant and the unpleasant), we rediscover the real depth of our experience. This is how we really become more conscious.

6

Reclaiming The Heart

So this human capacity to feel, this connection which puts us back in touch with the basic ground of our being or our 'true nature', that's really what we have always longed to know somewhere inside. If we don't recognise it, it is usually because we are deeply entrenched in the rabbit hole of ideas and mind, or have lost completely our capacity to feel.

I truly and deeply believe that it's worth fighting to stay conscious and not be numb, working to reclaim the deepest part of our heart and its capacity to feel.

None of us are inherently greedy or inherently angry or inherently selfish. What in truth we're missing is that deep connection to our heart, because when we do touch that place, when we are really in touch with the deepest part of us, we know that just being alive itself is full of wonder.

It's completely understandable that we feel something is lacking all the time, but we don't know where to look to find what we feel is missing. That search can go on for our whole life, and often does. When that connection is lacking in us, why would we think to look for it in a quiet moment where nothing of any particular interest is going on? It's quite possibly the last place we would look. But I want to say to you that whatever else you choose to do in your life, doing whatever you have to do to end that numbness is absolutely what you should do. Because I promise you when it's gone, your quest for meaning in your life will be over and you'll understand what you came here for.

When you find really what is the true nature of your being, what the ground for your life actually stands upon, regardless of what you think it is, you'll know that it doesn't matter where you are. You'll know that just to be alive is profoundly moving and deeply meaningful and extraordinary – and all the things you think you have to add to it, to make it something special, is only because you didn't spot what life actually is. But when you do find that, all of your needs will have been met, all of your confusion will be over, and you'll realise what an unbelievable, extraordinary thing it is that you're alive right now and how many unbelievable opportunities there are to do something with that life.

So I ask you to learn to stop and rest from time to time in the stillness of your own heart. Because behind the madness of what is going on all around you and within you it is that stillness which always rests in the background that connects you to everything and everyone.

The real thing that we have forgotten that is the cause for all this chaos that we get ourselves in is just the losing of that connection to what lies in the stillness when you really touch it deeply. It's not an empty space, my friends. It is an emptiness that contains that profound, unfathomable love that is the basis for everything you see around you all the time. And it's the basis for you.

Somewhere deep inside you know that that's in your heart, but you've just forgotten it, or you've just somehow found yourself in a state of disconnect. The answer is so much more simple than you might have thought it is. When you've found it again you'll know that all that's left to do in your life is to share the love that you find in that stillness with everybody you possibly can, in any way you possibly can, and that the things you thought you needed you really don't need. What you're supposed to do with your life is to be a testimony to what it is to actually really be a human being, to express it, to live it, so that those around you get a flavour of it, a taste of it.

We just can't have everything that we want, and we don't need everything. The only thing we really need is to know that we're connected to our own hearts, because that's how we are connected to everybody else around us, whether they are the most extraordinary human being on the planet, or the one in the greatest state of despair. When we're connected at our own heart we will know that we are connected to life and everything in it. And at that moment we will feel truly alive. And one thing about feeling truly alive is that no matter how much suffering there might be, behind that suffering there is a love so boundless and unwavering that is has the capacity to heal even our deepest wounds.

Now that's what we all came here for. To feel

and be touched by that love. So, if you have to work hard at developing your capacity to feel that connection then please don't give up. If you have to make choices and compromises, do so, but don't give up, and don't get disheartened, because although it might be a little harder than you had hoped, it is always worth fighting for. It is worth giving every ounce of your energy to. We will all have to make some choices and each of us will have to make an agreement with ourselves to stick at it and acknowledge that the life that we have is indeed precious, because it might be a long time before you get another crack at it.

Somewhere inside we all already know this, and it's only because we become so distracted with our lives that we forget.

* * *

Key Survival Point For Staying Conscious

There is more intelligence in the heart than there is in the brain. It is through the heart that we reconnect to the real intelligence behind life itself, something that may have confused us at a mental level for a long time. The love that lies in the background of our lives reveals itself gradually to our heart and not our mind, as we learn to feel deeply again. Do whatever it is you have to do to overcome whatever numbness you are feeling, however hard it might be.

(You might like to listen to the accompanying album Brave Souls, Track 8. Reclaim The Heart)

Part Two:

A Deeper
Look Within

7

Life Is Consciousness, Consciousness Is Life

It was the Buddha who originally pointed out that greed and aversion are not innate in any of us but simply conditioned responses that evolve within us. He suggested that the condition for the arising of greed, selfishness, anger and ill will is simply confusion, or ignorance. Simply, we become confused because we cannot see or understand what is going on. We don't see what life actually is. Our suffering, he suggested, is caused by our inability to pay sufficient attention to what is actually governing our lives.

So let's start now by looking at what we might not be paying attention to. And for that let's start right at the beginning, or if you like, let's start with the biggest, most obvious thing of all. Life - what is it?

It's going on around us everywhere, we are an expression of it ourselves, it is the basic principle that governs our entire experience of being. And yet for all of man's ingenuity it still remains to a large extent the most unfathomable mystery. Here we are on this planet, somewhere in the vastness of space, rotating yearly around the sun, on this earth which is rotating daily around its own axis, and we just wake up every day, not quite sure where we go to at night, carrying on without the slightest idea of what it is all about!

We have broken the parts of it down and looked at it under a microscope, we have analysed it and tried to make sense of just how the coming together of a sperm and an egg randomly sometime in the past produced each of us individually. And we haven't really come close to figuring that out.

Now I would say that instead of trying to reduce it down into its constituent parts and rob it of its exquisite mystery, we should allow it to be the very mystery that it is and start to acknowledge that perhaps there might be more to it than meets the eye. When we acknowledge that there might be more intelligence behind it than we have assumed, we create a space within our hearts where we allow ourselves to start to honour life as sacred again; deeply so.

Perhaps you haven't stopped for a while to reflect upon it, but this is your life, and it really is so special, and if you are suffering, unhappy or dissatisfied with it, it most certainly is worth doing whatever you can to turn that around and find your joy. This life really is so brief and taking the time to reflect on your own suffering and happiness is certainly worth your while.

We have spent a long, long time trying to figure this world out through scientific observation. The problem scientists have faced since they tried to unravel life's great mystery is that all they have had to observe was the apparent physically expressed form of it. We can only quantify, as science loves to do, that which we can discretely perceive to be there. By removing consciousness from the equation, we may have robbed life of the very sacredness which might prompt us to respect it and honour it more than we currently do.

From the late 1890's to the mid-1920's, after an exhaustive study of everything they could observe, a number of eminent scientists, Plank, Bohr and Einstein, amongst others, together some of the greatest intellectual minds in history, reached this milestone; they could no longer separate manifest reality from the consciousness that observed it. Although some scientists have gone on to conjecture about what this implies and propose that the universe is the workings of a deep intelligence, this opened a Pandora's box for science and it is not quite sure what to make of it.

Scientists have spent the last eighty years trying to understand the implications of this discovery which requires such a complex understanding of mathematics to mechanically fathom what has been realised. It is so baffling to the intellect that for the most part the implications it might have on our moral understanding of life have generally fallen prey to the efforts to use quantum theory in the development of increasingly complex technology. Meanwhile mainstream Western thinking has continued to adopt the view that this is simply a material universe and consciousness is an occasional by-product of material processes. The problem with this is that there is one great big elephant in the room the moment we even start down this root. And that is this:

Life itself *is* consciousness.
Consciousness *is* life.

It is consciousness that is the intelligent organising principle that galvanises life and brings it into expression. Any attempt to understand life in the absence of consciousness is going to fall hopelessly short. We have continued to adopt the ironically named C18th Western Enlightenment view that the universe is a material occurrence that under certain circumstances brings forth life. But what if, in truth, it was a conscious universe that under certain circumstances brings forth matter and expresses itself as life when this consciousness and matter interact? Perhaps that is a big step to take, so let's take it gently.

Taking a materialist approach to understand life is a bit like trying to understand your computer simply by looking at the hardware. When we take the actual physical thing apart and look inside and try to fathom how on earth it does all the myriad things it does, there is no way that by looking at the constituent parts we are going to figure out how it works. That is because the real functionality of the computer is governed not by its hardware, but by its software. It is the flow and current of information that brings it to life. We, the human being, indeed any form of life, is exactly the same.

Consciousness is the software package that brings this mass of flesh and bones to life. And it is the absence of it that marks us as dead. It is as simple as that. The appearance of consciousness within a living organism produces a subtle electromagnetic current or field. In fact all things that are alive are alive because of this subtle current that is produced by consciousness. It is this current that flows life through us, and the absence of it is death. It is important to understand that this current is not produced by the food we eat or the air that we breathe. It is produced by the consciousness that arises within us. Scientists may well just see this as an electrical charge, but it is a living flowing current of consciousness.

Science has for a long time known that we can communicate information through electromagnetic fields. This is how all of our wireless technology works. In the same way that our phone sends electromagnetic signals that carry information, so too our body and mind communicate endlessly through electromagnetism. It is not enough to see life as just an electrical current. We have to start to understand the information that it conveys.

If you ever watch a plant with your naked eye it's extremely hard to recognise the point at which it goes from being alive to the point at which it's dead. There's quite a long period when it's sort of almost alive, or barely alive, but it's still alive. And then there's a point where it's clearly not. In a human being it's much more obvious. There's a moment that marks the point of death, and although it doesn't look very different with the naked eye because the physical body remains intact, it has profoundly changed at an unseen level. So profoundly in fact that it is now no longer capable of performing any functions whatsoever.

And what is it that marks it as dead? The heart's stopped? Is that it? No. The mark – the sign of life in all things - is the appearance of this subtle field, this very, very delicate charge, or electro-magnetic field; this electrical charge is the current of life itself. The presence within the organism of this charge is what marks it as alive. The absence of it marks it as dead. That's it. And although there is very little change physically – you have to look quite hard to be sure that someone is dead, it's blatantly obvious when you can see that field of life within them and around them. With the withdrawal of consciousness from the body during the dying process that subtle electrical field fades. There is a point at which it is no longer able to support the heart and it stops beating, and thereafter a point where all activity, even of the brain and nerves, likewise ceases.

This field of life is produced by one thing, and only by one thing. It's produced by the arising of consciousness within the organism, by awareness itself. I am not talking about the kind of active intelligence that is produced by our brain, I am talking about the basic ground of our very being, which is consciousness or awareness itself. This is a pure intelligence that expresses itself absolutely perfectly for as long as it's allowed to. The integrity and coherence of this living, conscious current as it flows through us is one of the single most important conditioning factors behind the integrity of life itself.

One of the greatest challenges we now face is that we have learned to interfere with this living current of life so much that as a living organism we are starting to break down to an unprecedented degree. As I have said before, the huge increase in degenerative disease and psychological sickness is a testimony to how out of balance the human life has become. There is no other living organism that degenerates in such a huge variety of ways as does the human being.

The huge mistake we have made in exploiting the potential of our modern telecommunications is that we have totally failed to anticipate just how dramatically this disrupts some of the most delicate mechanisms by which life functions. We will look at this is much more detail in a subsequent chapter but I would like to start to introduce this subject here. When you send a text from your phone saying, "I love you" that message is actually encoded into a signal that is disruptive to our living energy field. When such a feeling arises within you at the point that you actually tell someone, "I love you" you convey that very feeling to the other person, not just through the words you speak but through the resonance that it creates in your energy field.

Once we start living in an environment that is totally dominated by unnatural electromagnetic signals, our living space becomes incoherent. This has dramatic implications for how we actually feel within ourselves, even if we are not yet able to recognise what it might be doing physiologically. Where before our feelings of love, empathy, anger and jealousy were carried within us and expressed right through us at the "felt" deepest level, the sheer level of chaotic "white noise electromagnetism" that we are living in these days means often that we simply don't know how we feel any more. We have literally traded the resonance of our inherent connectedness to a virtual/mental idea of connectedness. It is quite possibly one of the greatest paradoxes of our time, that while we believe ourselves to be more connected than ever, at the deepest level we are more disconnected than we have ever been. Once we get used to this way of functioning we will quickly forget that we ever had such an ability. Once we stop feeling the effects of what we do, say and think, our lives will become very two dimensional and it is highly likely that we will start to find our virtual world to be more compelling than our actual reality.

So perhaps we need to take seriously the implications of this unpoliced interference with the delicate and sacred nature of life itself. Nature expresses itself absolutely perfectly for as long as it is allowed to do so. Life is a pure response for as long as it's allowed to be so. The degree to which it is interfered with will always be reflected in the way in which it expresses itself. Since we, as humans, are governed by the same principles as all life and all of nature, we would likewise express ourselves absolutely perfectly for as long as we allow life to flow seamlessly through us.

It is the journey that reconnects us to our true nature that ends our sense of separation from what we are experiencing. This journey eventually takes us to a place where we can accept life for what it is and stop fighting with it. Although we might find it extremely challenging to let go our need to control life, we have to understand that it is not personal. Although we may need to seek some kind of personal resolution in order to feel able to let go, life itself is not a personal process. The universe does not behave differently for you than it does for anyone else. Taking it too personally is one of the greatest causes of our suffering.

Life itself is a singular process regardless of the myriad ways in which it expresses itself. It doesn't vary in the way in which it functions, however it may vary in the way it manifests or expresses itself. It is only ever a pure reflection of the conditions upon it. Although what we are experiencing is not personal, it is a personal opportunity to explore this extra-ordinary thing that is life. The danger of course is that we interfere so much with it in the process of exploring it that we may break that very sacred intelligence that is supporting us.

If we really do value consciousness as living beings, our greatest challenge is to honour the real intelligence of it and stop thinking that our intellect is capable of fully understanding it. Life has been going on for billions of years without anybody understanding anything about it and it has gone on perfectly. As we have evolved to become the most intelligent creatures on the planet we have also become the most interfering. Perhaps it is time to allow life to be as sacred as it truly is, and to honour and respect it as such?

* * *

Key Survival Point For Staying Conscious

The universe is conscious and alive and sacred by its very nature. It is our failure to recognise this that has allowed us to feel justified in the way in which we exploit it. When we learn to recognise that the whole universe is conscious, we recognise also that we are accountable for our actions. Learning to see that all life is sacred brings us back to a place of deep respect for it.

8

The Age of Individuality: When Consciousness Turns In On Itself

"People seldom do what they believe in.
They do what is convenient, then repent."
                                                    - Bob Dylan

The human life when viewed from a mechanical or materialist perspective has a certain evolutionary process of its own which we can simply observe happening. It starts with birth, the growth of the physical body, the development of our idea of ourself, the experience of living within the world and the gradual decay, the breaking apart of that towards the end of life and then finally, the death. It's a cycle of arising and passing away, just like everything in life is a cycle.

From the materialist perspective, life appears to be the expression of matter becoming conscious for a period and then unconscious. After death there is material residue that remains in the absence of consciousness. That's really what life basically appears to be when we simply observe it physically. The human consciousness as it emerges through the life, out of infancy, develops ever more complex ideas of itself as an individual. The degree to which the emergence of an individualised sense of self is instinctive or conditioned is a question of endless debate, but there is no doubt that this tendency becomes increasingly galvanised as we grow up through childhood and into adolescence. As this process runs its course our personality becomes a reflection of our efforts to convey or project our individualised sense of who we think we are out to the world.

Without any connection to a higher aspect of consciousness (be that through religious, devotional, spiritual enquiry, meditation or simply because we live in a natural environment in ways that develop a sense of connectedness), the idea of ourselves evolves. It is informed by our experiences and the influence of parents, friends, peer groups and our own imagination, as we relate personally to conditions that we meet. So we create this multi-layered sense of self that becomes highly individualised, and as far as we believe as humans at this time in history, highly evolved.

In the past few generations as a society we have reached the pinnacle of individuality. If we look at the influences upon us now, everything is pointing towards trying to express ourselves as individually as possible. Everything is galvanised around the idea of *'me'* as the unit; what I can display to the world and what kind of responses I can elicit. To a degree social media today reflects our obsession with this created idea of self and the need to feel seen by others. Of course it is also a reflection of our wish to express ourselves and share our experiences in some way, but the increased focus around the perception of self that is conveyed is clear to be seen. The selfie stick is a classic example of the feeling that it is we who need to hold centre stage and play the starring role.

As we grow up, one of the greatest pressures we feel under comes from our endless concerns around comparing ourselves to others and how we are compared by others. A significant sense of our personal worth comes from the feeling of being favourably compared to others, and our sense of inadequacy from comparing ourselves as less so (valuable, worthy, good, attractive, skilful, etc.). This insistence on comparing ourselves with others is pride, and when it becomes obsessive it leads to vanity and even narcissism.

This pride is both the habitual comparison of our self to others, as well as the comparison of our experience, as better, same or worse than our ideas of how we think it should be. It is the single biggest contributing factor to our sense of separation and distance from what we are experiencing and to the isolation we feel from those around us. In effect, our need to be different, and individual, creates a conscious separation from others. The more we obsess about our idea of ourselves, the more withdrawn into our projected but inner world we become. Often it becomes the case that we end up relating more to our ideas of what is happening to us than the actual experiences we have themselves. I often call this our "I-making extravaganza", because in many of us, the effort put forth to uphold and project our individual sense of self becomes the single biggest galvanizing force within our lives.

The effect of all this has been that the human idea of itself has evolved in isolation or separate from its relationship to life more generally and to the environment we live in. We have found ways to express ourselves outside of our relationship to the natural order and cycles. In our intoxication with the things that we have created we have cut ourselves off more and more from the creative principles and natural intelligence that is actually governing our lives.

In spite of all this, the human being still appears to be the most 'evolved' expression of life. Most other life evolves only to the point of being sexually aware, with that sexual polarity, in combination with the survival instinct, being the galvanizing energy that drives it. As humans, the sexual energy and the desire to procreate is also the strongest motivating energy in life, and even more so when life stops being a daily struggle for survival. Even the desire to accumulate more possessions and status is largely governed by the fact that by being stronger or more elaborate and appealing in our display, we will attract the best mate. Desire, and in particular sexual desire, *is* the very force behind our lives. 'Desire for' something in itself is not the cause of suffering, but what lies behind our desires and the degree to which we are driven by them is.

For all the intricacies of the human psyche it still remains that when we try to deconstruct life by merely observing the ways in which it expresses itself materially, we tend to come to the belief that life is just a rare occurrence of matter becoming conscious under certain circumstances. It is all too easy to come to this view because there isn't any hint, when we look at it under a microscope, that there may be any more to life than that. So it's understandable that we should come to the conclusions we do. As I said earlier, this has been the view of mainstream science and materialists for quite some time. It has been the predominant view around which most modern societies have organised themselves. It isn't until we come back up from our microscope and start to look around us at the extraordinary display of life again with eyes wide open that we become humbled enough to remember that it is still an awe inspiring mystery in all of its unfathomable beauty.

However, in our 'human-centric' world where we forget what we are actually a part of, here we are, in our life, working very hard to establish our position, vying for it, negotiating it, fighting for it, standing up for it, struggling to uphold it. After a period of turbulent and rapid growth and develop-ment we reach a stage in our late twenties when we become mature as an adult. The growth phase reaches a peak; the vital forces have already peaked and our mental capacities have likewise started to reach a peak. We may choose to sit down and train them but the process of growing up is complete. Following this, the process of ageing and decay begins.

So there we are. We have gone through the painful process of creating this idea of ourselves and now there lies ahead of us the rest of our lives in which to express that idea to the world. So off we go seeking friendships, partnerships and positions, engaging in experiences that express and uphold this idea of me. Then, somewhere along the line, it dawns upon us. "Whoa, hold on a minute! The process of growth and expansion that I've been utterly immersed in is now not expanding any more". And we look to the future and we realise there will be a time in the future where we are going to die.

It is all too common to have an existential crisis as we look ahead and reflect upon the inevitability of death. And yet we doggedly continue to try and hold the idea of ourselves together. Often, even in our hospital bed when we're told we only have a month to live, we desperately try to hold this idea of ourselves together, trying to find a way out of the predicament we find ourselves in. The predicament that everything we have invested our entire life in is about to be stripped away. And at that point, quite often, people start to pray, start to ask for spiritual guidance or open up in some way.

So life runs its course and the gradual onset of old age begins to nudge us towards entertaining the idea of letting go. Maybe it is because we can't move physically as much as we used to, or we can't do as much as we used to, we can't gather as much energy around us as we used to, and we can't project ourselves out into the world with as much force and dynamism as we used to. So there is a process of having to relinquish as we begin to reflect upon our apparent demise. And hopefully we acknowledge that this life is going to come to an end, inevitably.

But what is going to come to an end? It is my idea of myself and the personal and individual expression that I have spent my whole life orchestrating that will come to an end. And so, without any spiritual context to our life, never having reflected upon whether there might be anything beyond this or having ignored, denied or refused to accept the possibility that there even might be, we face our end.

The process by which the living universe is produced by consciousness reveals itself gradually over time through deep meditation and the insight that arises as we observe the creative process within us and around us. This is one of the processes that the Buddha himself acknowledged was hard to perceive and hard to grasp. But it is the experience of this, or the coming to understand this in some way, which prompts us to reject the purely materialist approach to life. This marks the beginning of the journey beyond the veil of appearances, to glimpse and connect to the intelligence that lies behind them. Of course, the notion or conviction that there might perhaps be more to life than this purely physiological/material process that we are able to observe, frequently does also arise in many of us as an act of faith, conjecture or imagination. The notion of a creative intelligence behind our lives has arisen in us as humans since the dawn of time and in every culture and civilisation. The one we are currently living in is the only significant one that lacks a spiritual perspective as the basis for its world view. The question we need to be asking ourselves is whether the removal of such a perspective has led to a development and evolution in us as conscious beings or not.

The human life when looked at without a spiritual context may lead us to the very convenient conclusion that, "Yes, none of my actions have any real consequences because I'm here for just a brief time, and when I'm gone, I'm gone". It's the perfect invitation to selfishness. And so off we go indulging ourselves in the pursuit of everything we can hope to bring our way, assuming that life is all about getting as much out of it as we can because it's just curtains when we die. Of course the recognition that others may be affected by our actions often acts as a check to what might otherwise become purely selfish inclinations, and rightly so, but we often fail to reach a point of personal accountability that sees that our own wellbeing is deeply defined by the actions we take and the volition that prompts them.

So what does a world look like inhabited largely by beings who take this materialist stance on life? Well, basically, it looks like the world we see around us right now. Although we can observe clearly the effects of our actions upon others and the world around us, and in spite of the fact that we know categorically we have been taking out more than we put in at alarming rates, we remain reluctant to significantly reduce our consumption. The pull towards the pursuit of our desires and the continued projection of ourselves out to the world for personal gain prompts us to pretend to ourselves, at both an individual and group level, that we haven't seen what's happening in order to justify our continued pursuits.

It isn't that we are stupid. We are intelligent. But the Buddha did not claim that suffering was caused by stupidity, he said it was caused by ignorance. Ignorance is the willingness to ignore or not pay attention to how things are. That is the real cause of suffering. The question is what are we not paying attention to? Not only are we not paying attention to what is going on around us (something that we can choose to ignore if we wish), we are also not paying attention to how we *feel*! In our increasing numbness we are able to witness things that instinctively would upset, move or disturb us.

The point here is that consciousness does not just tend towards the selfish projection of ourselves upon the world. There are deeper human feelings that arise within us such as love, compassion and empathy that are anything but selfish responses to the world. They are all prompted by a deep feeling of connected-ness to something that is beyond this idea of myself. All of the highest of human qualities, like love, compassion and empathy, are borne of a sense of connection. The more galvanised around self view we become, the more they are choked of the vital energy that they are borne of. It is when we stop feeling these things that we find the grounds to pursue our desires selfishly.

When one who is 'view-rooted' looks out upon the material universe and witnesses things like love and compassion, they come to the view that they are the response of beings trying to make sense of their life or add meaning to their personal perspective. Likewise, they would argue that our ideas of a creative intelligence behind life, or the tendency to form religious ideas of God, are merely ideas produced in the mind that serve the purpose of trying to make life feel meaningful when it is not inherently so.

One who is 'experience-rooted' feels what is

happening within them and around them, recognising that we are all sharing a common experience (i.e. the experience of being alive). Likewise, they start to recognise that we are connected at a much deeper level than we may appear to be, and that our thoughts and ideas are merely things we add to our experience but that they are not the experience itself.

Our capacity to feel deeply for each other is in no way a cerebral process but a deeply embodied *felt* experience. When we start to pay enough attention at an experiential level to what is going on within us and around us, rather than trying to figure it all out at the level of ideas, gradually we witness the dismantling of our isolated sense of self. With this comes the gradual emergence or recognition of a profound intelligence behind our lives, through which we are all deeply connected to each other. This inner conviction does not come upon us because we join up the dots or put all the pieces of the jigsaw together. It comes through at a much deeper level than that of our concrete ideas.

In fact, we may spend most of our lives not fully understanding how or why we feel the way we do, but simply knowing that we do. Scientifically we have not been able to explain the level at which we might be connected beyond recognising that we share a common ancestry. But one of the most compelling of all spiritual experiences, and one that happens repeatedly to each of us in meditation, when we begin to really pay attention to what we are experiencing, is the absolute conviction that we are deeply connected to each other and to all of life. It is this experience more than anything else that dissolves in us any previous willingness to act harmfully or selfishly in the pursuit of our personal desires and ambitions. This experience of connectedness, and the dissolving of our egoic focus upon ourselves as an individual that it produces, works to temper our behaviour and attitude towards life and others more convincingly than any moral code we may have been asked to subscribe to. It is the gradual coming to this resolution within ourselves that brings about what the Buddha called the "cessation of suffering and its causes".

In short, the more connected to our true nature we are, the less we bring ourselves to suffering. The more separated from it, the more suffering we cause and experience.

* * *

Key Survival Point For Staying Conscious

When we stop comparing ourselves to others and fixating on our need to be seen, we recognise that our real needs are far fewer than we think. The more elaborate is our idea of ourself, the less easily we find contentment and happiness. Try to notice just how much your idea of yourself imposes itself on what you do, and see how much freer you would be to dance with life once you start to let the ego go.

9

The Cost of Convenience

"It's a crazy world we're living in...
...Futures made of virtual insanity now
Always seem to, be governed by this love we have
For useless, twisting, our new technology
Oh, now there is no sound - for we all live
   underground"

- Jamiroquai, Virtual Insanity

I am convinced that the way we currently use technology, and the nature of that technology itself, is having serious implications upon our mental, emotional and physical wellbeing. I am of course aware of just how much people value technology in their lives but I have no doubt that the effect of wireless technology on the way we function consciously is far more significant than has currently been acknowledged. So not to include the material in this chapter I felt would be a disservice to the reader. I can only apologise if it upsets some of you that I would be making such suggestions. I am well aware that scientific proof in support of what I am saying is only just starting to emerge. But it is emerging and the reports that are coming through are becoming increasingly more alarming. I am not going to look now at the physiological effects of wireless technology. I want to investigate the way in which technology is changing the way we function at the level of consciousness.[5]

So let's talk about consciousness and technology and the ways in which technology has changed the way we function at a conscious level. Consciousness is the perception of, or our awareness of, our experience. The mechanism by which we feel and register this experience is through a very delicate electro-magnetic field that moves within us at all times, as I investigated earlier. Actually, this is your life field or life force, if you like to call it that. We are in effect electrical beings, and the integrity of our whole being depends deeply upon the integrity and coherence of our subtle electro-magnetic field. As the coherence of our subtle electrical current becomes disrupted, so the depth and texture of our experience gradually gets diluted.

As living organisms, as living beings, we naturally come into resonance with what is going on around us. There is a natural principle at work that expresses itself within our own living bio-electromagnetic field, and this is one of the key factors that marks us as actually being alive rather than dead, again as I touched on earlier. Always and everywhere,

5   Debating the science behind the effects of EMR (Electromagnetic Radiation) on human health is not the purpose of this book. If you are not aware of the current scientific developments in this field of the effects of EMR I would strongly recommend that you read *Overpowered* by *Martin Blank PhD* for a detailed look at this subject as I feel this is important enough of an issue to inform ourselves on. Interestingly at the time of going to print in the most recent study a $25m project (May 2016) by the US Federal Agency the National Toxicology Program found a link between RF-EMR and cancer in rats. This federal agency is trying to work out how to inform the public about these new findings.

in order to make us feel comfortable, our own living electromagnetic energy field, that is the very carrier of our experience of life, moment to moment, is constantly reorganising itself to come into coherence with the environment in which we find ourselves in.

Now twenty years ago there were not so many man-made electromagnetic fields in our environment, and so our default setting was to constantly come back into resonance with the natural field of energy produced by our planet and the life going on around us; this living bio-field of energy that we call nature. The planet has its own coherence, its own magnetic field, its own electromagnetic field. Everything in nature produces its own coherent energy field, just as we do as human beings. One of the principles that keeps our life in balance is the fact that we are a small electromagnetic field in a much bigger one and simply by existing in it and moving through it, the integrity of this bigger field has the capacity to bring us back naturally to coherence when we expose ourselves to it. This is one of the reasons we feel so refreshed simply by being out in nature, and why we feel heavy and numb if we spend too much time in an unnatural environment.

Now in the last ten or fifteen years we have started to add new energy fields to the equation. We have started to produce electromagnetism at much greater levels than we would naturally be exposed to and many of us are now living in those electromagnetic fields, often for twenty-four hours a day, many of us. So if we go back only a few years, back to the early 80's, living in London or New York, the same hustle and bustle, the same noise, and the same pollution - maybe the pollution is actually less these days - the one thing that wasn't there was the ubiquitous use of mobile phones. There was little wireless technology and hence there were far less microwaves. So even though we were in a city full of concrete, full of cars, full of noise, we were still in a natural ambient environment. The pervading ambient energy field was of nature. Even though we couldn't see much nature around us, it was there in the background. Nowadays we are living in a new ambient energy field that was not there before. Some of us are exposed to it for twenty-four hours of every single day, because we never switch off our own devices.

The question we need to be asking ourselves is what does this exposure actually entail? A mobile phone uses energy to transmit data from one point to another. To get information from one point to another point without a cable, you need to use a pulse of energy. This energy is an electromagnetic pulse, or as it is called technically, electromagnetic radiation (EMR). This charge, or pulse of energy, produced by any wireless device, will subtly interfere with any other electrical system near it. This is a law of physics. The human brain and nervous system is an electrical system, as I have said. Given that the human electrical system functions in the range of millivolts and phones and other wireless devices operate in the range of volts, these devices are thousands of times more powerful than the subtle electromagnetic systems of a human being. While scientists are still trying to work out what cumulative effect this is having upon our nervous systems, I strongly feel it would be prudent to be cautious about the level to which we are willing to expose ourselves to these technologies.

It took forty years to make a valid case against tobacco and asbestos. The collateral damage in that period was immense. Since that time a 'Precautionary Principle' has been introduced and is a prerequisite before any medical substance is sanctioned for human consumption. What it says is that no substance should be allowed for human consumption until it is proved to be safe. It alarms me that exposure to man-made EMR has been allowed at a completely unpoliced level while the long term effects upon our health have yet to be adequately explored. The dramatic increase in our exposure to man-made EMR has only happened in the last 5-10 years and already there are alarming signs that it is detrimental to our health. Even tobacco and asbestos didn't show convincing health risks in such a short period of time as this. While scientists continue to try to quantify the effects of our recent exposure to man-made EMR, surely we could start to reflect that it is going to be disruptive to something as delicate as the subtle electrical life currents produced by our consciousness.

We as humans are relatively robust forms of life and so the effects of EMR upon us may take time to become apparent. But this summer I was staggered to realise that as I sat out on my porch at night in the Mediterranean, I was not bothered by mosquitoes and not one moth was flitting around the lamp on the wall. It wasn't long ago that I would have needed either a mosquito net or a coil to sit as undisturbed as this. Furthermore we are already hearing worrying reports that bee colonies are collapsing and certainly it seems that the more delicate creatures are being hugely effected by the now massive impact that our man-made electro-pollution is having upon them.

I think one of the reasons that we are so slow to pick up on this is that we can't see this subtle field of information that is produced by consciousness, any more than we can see the software that makes our computer function when we look at the box in which it is running. Our subtle energy field is not apparent to us when we look at the physical body or even when we cut it up, so it is all too easy for doctors and scientists to come to the conclusion, "Well, our bodies don't appear to be changing much when we use this technology".

We have to ask ourselves subtler questions and not just gross questions like, "Is this electro-magnetic field emitted by mobiles and wifi etc. heating my cellular body up? Is it producing changes in my DNA and in my cellular structure?" Although there is already evidence emerging that it is, we actually have to ask ourselves simple questions: "How do I feel now that I have been using high speed wifi and 4G phones for the past few years? How do I feel these days when I spend six hours in my office, as opposed to ten years ago spending six hours in my office? How do I feel now when I take the tube to work, compared to how I felt taking the tube to work ten years ago? How do I feel now when I sit in a library reading a book, compared to how I felt ten years ago sitting in a library reading a book?"

Well, we might feel very different without having noticed, or if we have noticed, we may not have understood why. It may have not even occurred to us to notice how we feel and we may have to stop and start to pay attention to notice it at all. But I'll bet a lot of us, when we ask ourselves honestly, would probably admit that we don't feel as still, settled or as comfortable within ourselves as we might have done ten years ago.

Back then when we walked into the library, the only thing going on there was people sitting quietly reading books, and it often felt like quite a refuge, a peaceful and relaxing place to be. It might even, at times, feel like a sacred space on account of the absence of all the normal noise and activities we humans get up to most of the time. Now you go into a library today and it's full of people sitting quietly, reading books (often on a computer screen), but that's not all - it will be full of different electromagnetic fields from multiple wifi routers, mobile phones, wifi hotspots, fire alarm systems, intruder alarm systems, heating controls, computer systems and much more. Altogether this is bombarding our working spaces with electro-magnetism and the chaotic information it is carrying. It is important that we understand that these electromagnetic fields have no intelligence to them, and far from being supportive in the way the natural ambient fields are, they are highly disruptive.

As a meditation teacher I see, and I am sure many others like therapists and doctors are seeing, a huge increase in the number of people suffering with depression, suffering with anxiety, exhaustion and sleep disorders, as well as large numbers of children suffering with the inability to concentrate or a deficiency in their capacity to pay attention. Do we really think that this just happened to happen? Do we really think that it just was an accident that these things are increasing at exponential rates? At alarming rates that we have never seen before, at exactly the same rate that we have increased our exposure to man-made electromagnetic fields and signals, which were not in our lives just a few years ago?

Now, I understand how much convenience it has brought to us, that we can sit almost anywhere and catch up with our emails, communicate with our friends, download the latest news or even watch any movie we could choose. But what is the cost of bringing that much convenience into our lives? Was it really that inconvenient that I had to go to a particular chair or to a particular desk or to a particular part of my room to sit down and do my emails? Even without wireless technology and just a simple cable (ethernet) plugin, within a few seconds of wanting it, I had access to almost all the information I could possibly imagine.

I can feel what this technology is doing to us probably because I meditate; perhaps I am a little more sensitive to it than some. But the fact that people cannot feel it is actually the alarming thing. What part of us is it that actually has to shut down so that we don't feel this mass of man-made electromagnetism that we are constantly exposed to?

Well, it is exactly the same part of us that feels all the richness of our experience, all its subtlety; a feeling of deep appreciation when we watch a beautiful sunset, or the feeling of empathy when we sit and discuss something meaningful with somebody else. It's the same part that allows us to feel compassion when we look upon someone who is struggling or love when we reflect upon someone dear to us. These deeper feelings, these flavours of our experience, they are all happening in that very narrow bandwidth that feels all that richness and all the subtlety. We have to shut down so that we can't feel the subtle area of our energy field which is so disrupted as a result of what we are exposing ourselves to.

People come on meditation retreats. They take a two and a half hour journey out to the country and in twenty-four hours they tell me they are feeling so much better. I don't actually have to teach them meditation. I don't even have to tell them to do anything. There are no phones and no wifi signals when we are on retreat. It is just a clear and empty space. If they were just left in that space where they can actually start to reorganise and to allow their subtle electrical field, which is the energy of our life itself, to reorganise and to decompress from what it is exposed to, they would relax and start to open up again. The feeling of coherence that starts to return when we are undisturbed - this alone makes us feel much more settled within ourselves. We really do 'unwind'.

So here we are today, running around, chasing more and more stimulation. We have become stimulation-addicted because that's where we think our pleasure lies. We have lost our ability to sit quietly with ourselves and enter deeply into a simple moment, being undistractedly with ourselves, where we can feel totally connected with what's going on around us. It's sad really because there once was a time when such a moment was one of the most meaningful experiences there is.

So ask yourself if this convenience that we have sought through ever faster wireless signals, ever more powerful mobile devices and the electro-magnetic fields that it has required us to live in, ask whether it really is doing us a service or a disservice? And ask yourself what are you really prepared to pay for that convenience? Or perhaps ask it a different way: "Would you be willing to be inconvenienced a little bit in order to get back what we are starting to lose?"

Now there is another side to this story, and that is an expression of basic physics. And that is that two bodies in close proximity to each other come naturally into resonance with each other and become stable. What this means is that we feel more stable when we are in resonance with the ambient energy fields around us, regardless of whether they are the supportive ones of nature or the disruptive ones from our technology. Your body has to come into resonance with its environment otherwise we feel very uncomfortable. What this means is that once we are exposed to these fields, even though they are disruptive at a deeper level, we actually feel more comfortable when we are in resonance with them than when we are not. This is why, when you go away to the country or the seaside for a week, you feel exhausted when you arrive and gradually feel refreshed as the week goes by. You probably feel a kind of withdrawal syndrome and find yourself reaching for your phone or going online even without needing to or particularly wanting to. A similar effect is experienced by people coming out of the city to our retreats.

The problem with this is that when you go back to work in the city again the following week, you feel really unsettled because you are now in resonance with the environment you have just left behind. The first few days back at work and you are feeling, "Phew…just don't know if I can do this much longer". But a week later you are back in tune with the city and you start to feel normal again. Why do you feel OK again? Because you have brought yourself back to resonance with the ambient energy around you, but to do so you have to become numb again.

If your energy is high, coherent and wide open, and you are in a really dense and incoherent energy field, you are going to feel sick. It actually doesn't feel right, it feels wrong. So in order to feel OK again, your electrical field has to come into resonance with the ambient electrical fields around you, otherwise you just feel unwell, or unbalanced. Now you are in tune with your environment again, but what is the ambient energetic quality of your environment and is it bringing you into your highest state of possible health? You start to feel OK again, but have you reflected that perhaps you may have lost that magical sense of connection that you were starting to feel again on holiday?

This is happening all the time. To make that magical sense of connection we have to allow ourselves to tune up because that sense of connection is happening in the subtlest part of our field of perception. It is that part of us that is overwhelmed when we go back into London or any other city, and we feel, "Whoooaaa, that really stings". At that point our energy field shrinks and closes down again so that we feel overwhelmed. But in shutting down we lose that magical feeling of connectedness that we had before. I realise that this is a subtle point, and it is difficult to get this point across in a compelling way, so I can only ask you to reflect upon it for yourselves.

For me this is one of the greatest challenges of the modern age, because what we are losing touch with is the bit that actually makes us most human, and that is our ability to really recognise that connection, that deep empathy with those around us, that deep feeling of appreciative joy when we connect to what we are a part of. Those are the peak experiences that make us feel completely alive. Everything else we are chasing is a compensation for the bit we are missing. We *do* miss that feeling of connectedness, we miss it dearly even if we haven't realised it. How else could you explain the phenomena of social media if it is not for our longing for a sense of connection? It's a paradox in the truest sense of the word. We are more connected than we have ever been, and at the same time less connected than ever before.

As I said, it took forty years to make a case against tobacco and asbestos, by which time the damage was done. We can all choose to not smoke or use asbestos in our roofs, but the problem with EMR exposure is that we can't easily avoid it even if we wanted to. Which is why there is an emerging desire amongst people to take a digital detox, by going away and spending time where there is no wifi or mobile phone signals.

If I was to go back fifteen years to what it felt like when I sat and meditated, and this isn't because my meditation isn't on a par with where it was then, I can tell you that the subtlest, most exquisite part is not what it was then. I could feel the damage in my subtle body and the effects that that has upon my feelings of empathy and appreciation. It took me more than two years to repair that damage once I recognised what had happened.

So to get really in touch with the true potential of what it is to be a human being, which is the profound depth of the experiences we are capable of having, it's not just a question of spiritual enquiry, it's a question of repairing and nurturing, developing and taking care of this mechanism by which we are having those experiences. Because at the moment, for the most part, we are not taking care of it. Maybe we are doing our yoga, eating better, starting to meditate. We are not watching as much television, we're engaging in more intelligent conversation, we are doing all the right things, but we are doing them with our field of perception highly compromised because we are doing it in environments with a poor energetic quality to them.

The Buddha would have looked at it pragmatically. He would tell us that we are basically experiencing the effects of past choices. We chose such convenience over greater welfare. In order to have more and more convenience, and a more and more compelling virtual experience, we have bent the envelope more and more and more.

To get what we want, as quickly as we could

possibly have it, we have been willing to jeopardise or compromise our wellbeing. But let's not pretend to ourselves that there isn't a cost to bending the natural order to our will.

* * *

Key Survival Point For Staying Conscious

Ask yourself whether all the conveniences we have added to our lives have actually improved the satisfaction we get out of it. How much has all of this convenience contributed to the numbness we are feeling?

Reflect upon what might have been the real cost of convenience.

10

The Long Out Breath

I believe one of the greatest errors in recent history is the idea that the solution to the problems we face lies in growth. The assumption is that we need more and hence consistent growth and that a state of growth is the only relevant scenario for global development. This has been the standard economic model in developed nations since the Great Depression. Since then this has informed all mainstream thinking globally, from nation states to economists, social policy makers to corporations along with just about everybody else. This model is *fundamentally* flawed: you cannot have infinite growth in a finite system. There is no mileage left in this idea and in truth it is impossible to achieve, as nothing in the universe has grown or ever will grow forever.

All life, all living systems are cyclic. Everything that comes into being in time will pass away. There are three discrete stages of life. There is the arising, growth or coming into being stage. There is the resting, standing or just being state (where having arisen, life sustains itself under its own momentum for a while). Then there is the stage of gradual decay or passing away. Within life itself there are cycles, times of expansion and growth, times of rest and regeneration, times of contraction.

All of nature is governed by this cyclic way of things, even down to our very breath itself which is a constant process of taking in and giving back. For as long as life has existed on our planet, all of it has done so within a natural order that maintained a perfect balance. For all the life that appeared here, none of it had a net detrimental effect on the whole. Everything came and went without disturbing the great cycle of things. Teeming with life for hundreds of millions of years the planet remained pristine and unsullied or fatigued by the myriad forms of life it supported.

If we look we can see this cycle in everything - beings, plants, societies, planets, stars, all material things, everything. We can see this everywhere and it is not hard to see. And it's a cycle. Like the breath is a cycle. Expansion and contraction, this is the way of things. And it keeps a net balance by being like that. The universe does not exist in a state of conflict.

There's a point in our lives where we've reached a place where we're not going to grow any more. We've become a mature adult and we've reached a standing state. It is a point where we might stop taking for granted the fact that we will be supported and hopefully also reach the place where we stop taking out more than we contribute. In other words, having taken out a tremendous amount of resource to come to our state of personal maturity, there comes a time where, if our presence is not to become a detriment to the whole, we would need to put back into the system. We would need to contribute in some way to the pool which we have previously drawn from. And then towards the end of our life, we might hope to have given back to the world something of what we have taken out. In so doing we would have lived our life within the balance of the natural cycles of life.

The growth of communities, civilisations, groups of beings, has exactly the same intelligence to it. They grow, they become more complex, they form and organise themselves. The co-operation and coherence that it takes to create stability comes to a point, and at that point, if the moral compass has remained intact, then beings could reach a point of being able to delight in the stability that comes with the ending of the struggle for survival. If then they recognise that there are limits to what the planet can comfortably afford to provide, one would hope not only that they would regulate the level at which they choose to consume, but also, as an expression of gratitude, look for ways to give back to life.

The problem arises of course when we lose our sense of connection to the whole, and instead develop this self or 'individually' focused outlook that I investigated earlier, thus failing to consider the impact of our choices upon the whole. Likewise once we become accustomed to not having to struggle daily to support ourselves it is easy to take for granted, and even develop a sense of entitlement towards, all the things that have cost dearly for us to have along the way. We might even come to the point of believing that the planet and the rest of life is here simply to fulfil our own needs and desires, and for us to do with as we choose.

But regardless of the attitude that we might develop towards life, the same principles of expansion and contraction, growth and decay, of taking and giving back also hold true at a micro level within any living organism and within any structure. If it does not remain within the basic state of self-regulating balance it becomes unstable. As humans we rely on breath for life. We breathe in air that we need to sustain our life. But we don't just breathe in, do we? For every in breath there is an out breath. There is a point where if we keep breathing in, it doesn't feel very comfortable, and if we keep breathing in we start to do ourself a mischief, and if we still don't breathe out, we go pop! That is the way of things. If we don't breathe out when we need to we hold a tremendous amount of conflict, and friction and tension inside us. If we don't let life breathe the way it needs to breathe, we live with a tremendous amount of friction and tension, or life momentarily exists in a state of tension. There's a point where that becomes oppressive and then there is no longer any ground for the delight that comes naturally from existing within a natural state of balance.

So why am I saying this? I think somewhere deep down most of us accept that the way the modern world is rolling out doesn't feel quite right. For all the opportunity and convenience we have, somewhere, if we are willing to acknowledge it, many of us feel that something is misaligned even if we don't know what that is. We have transitioned out of the cycle of the 'Long *In* Breath' and failed to anticipate the change of approach that is now required. It is time to bring ourselves back into balance with the natural order and build our vision for the future of humanity around the notion of the '*Out* Breath'. This requires us to think of our lives in terms of contribution and not accumulation. We have dined out on our good fortune but our account is dangerously low on credit. It is surely time to put something back.

What happens when we keep taking out beyond this point where we've already got enough as a whole society? What happens is that we find ourselves in a state similar to the one where we are trying to breathe in when we're already full. It makes us sick. And if it never occurs to us to breathe out, well - it starts going wrong. It collapses. So each one of us can only be little a part of this world. But I would suggest that to think that the solution to our global problems comes in finding new areas of growth is mistaken. As I suggested, it's grown enough.

I would suggest that for us, if we look around us, the time for breathing out is now! In truth the in breath is actually the hardest part: the coming into being. The time of resting and breathing out should be the time of deep appreciation and delight. A time for seeking a deeper meaning and connection to life that only comes about when the struggle to stay alive momentarily ends.

So when we look to the world and wonder how we are going to engage in it now, in this time that we are living in, perhaps it is not so wise to look back to how recent generations before us engaged in it, because they were still trying to find comfort and stability in a world in which the out-take was not yet too far in excess of the input. The contribution of those generations to society and the human life has been done. The growth period and the forming of complex structures for most modern societies has happened. We were fortunate enough to have been born into the time where we could have stood upon the growth and development that has gone before, contributed to it and delighted in what it is to be one of those rare beings that are born in a time that is free of conflict, with the ease and the opportunity to engage in life and appreciate it.

Of course there are places where development hasn't been done and life is still a struggle for survival, but here in our modern societies it has. There is enough for everybody. There are those with more than enough and those with only just enough, and even in our fortunate societies there are those with not enough to live a life free of vexation. But there is enough to go round if beings are willing to share. So perhaps it is time to stop asking for more. If we keep asking for more and keep taking out then we are a part of that breath that is no longer possible, the breath that is already full. It's not possible to breathe in any more. When those who have enough don't say that's enough, and don't start thinking about putting back, there definitely isn't room for those who don't yet have enough to keep breathing.

So this is where we have come to. This is the world we are born into and will live our lives in. When we look at the natural order of things, we see things breathing in, and we see there are things breathing out. There are things coming into being and there are things passing away, all the time and everywhere. And that's why it stays for billions of years in a state of balance.

I would like you all to stop for a moment and do a very simple exercise for me.

Sit upright and breathe in for the count of 6. Then breathe out. I bet it feels nice. A good deep breath in and then a long out breath feels something of a relief to the system.

Now breathe in for the count of 10 and then breathe out (slowly and gradually breathe out so that you can relax and enjoy your out breath). Nice? Are some of you struggling to breathe in for 10? No doubt.

Now try again...breathe in for 10... and then in for 2 more...and another 2...
(Anyone still breathing in? Good lungs!!!)

Now breathe out. Slowly. Try to relax and enjoy the out breath. How many of you had to literally gasp out your breath, maybe with your head spinning and your ears wringing?

Finally breathe in as long as you possibly can...and then...keep breathing in.

How does *THAT* feel? And equally importantly, how does the out breath feel when it comes? Probably no longer able to enjoy and savour the release of tension that comes with a long sigh out, but no doubt relieved that you did!

Now just for a moment reflect on how eight billion people would feel if they all did the exercise you have just done at the same time!!!

So, maybe our progress now, our evolution, lies in finding a blissful way of breathing out. Because if we are honest with ourselves we will see that there is only a peace to be found in breathing out now, and this peace involves putting back, and letting go, and not holding on or taking out.

It may well be that some of us are in the place of the standing state where we could rest and stay there and be, and that's fine. Because there is that moment, and it's an exquisite moment when everything is just there, when it stands upon its own momentum, neither growing nor passing away. When we let go our perceived need to be moving forward always in search of more, we recognise that this is actually the most magical and fulfilling period of life. In order to appreciate it totally we have to also be willing to be with the growth and the passing away that are entailed in getting to that momentary state of being. If we can't embrace everything that it means to come into being, which is being born, growing, decaying and dying, then we won't yet be at peace with what it is to be alive.

Beyond the standing state, the letting go as we reach the zenith of our life and allowing ourself to unwind is not in itself suffering. When we are in alignment with what is happening to us, there is a bliss every bit as powerful in that experience, the experience of giving back and letting go, as there is in the experience of taking out.

It's important for us to reflect upon and seek to learn when we've had what's coming to us and delight in the fact that it came...and saying thank you, reflect upon what it is that we could put back, so that the same opportunity might come to those who follow.

Surely this is the only basis for a mature human society which seeks the genuine long term wellbeing of is people?

Things are going to breathe out. Humanity is going to breathe out one way or another. Breathing out can be a huge sigh of relief or it could be a point at which we expire! Our life ends with an out breath. So we hold it in our hands as to whether we are going to learn to delight as much in breathing out as we delighted in breathing in, or whether failing to do so becomes our undoing.

And that's where we are. This is our truth if we look honestly. We have been born here and are alive in this time. We didn't come here at another time to learn something else; somewhere in the past or in the future. We came here now, and this is a time to breathe out.

So I strongly suggest that we embrace wholeheartedly the idea of doing so. Because in it could be found a bliss I would even say far greater than the bliss of breathing in. The bliss of delighting in just being alive and knowing that we might contribute in some way as an expression of gratitude for all that life is. Whether or not we learn to do this will be the making or the undoing of us as a race, and in time will be the testimony to our success or failure as a species.

Now, some of you reading this are still young, so you're still breathing in within your life. But perhaps even then you may entertain the notion that your attitude to life will need to be, in aggregate, an out breath and not an in breath, because that's the time that we are in. Some of us have reached the stage where we've breathed in what we need to breathe in this life and have had what's coming to us. There is a delight in recognising that and seeing that it is enough, and allowing ourselves to breathe out.

There is no greater misery than reaching the end of your life still trying to breathe in. Or watching yourself grow old still trying to breathe in. To be alive and at peace with it is to embrace everything there is about life. So within the cycle of our own individual life, we need to understand that there will be a time to breathe in, a time of standing upon the foundations that our growing up has provided, and an equal period of out breath to make sure your life is a life of balance by the end of it. But within the greater cycle of life, and the cycle of humanity, we need to acknowledge that we are entering a time where we will need to learn to breathe out more than we currently do if we wish to find a peace between our life and the greater life unfolding all around us. If we get behind that rather than fight against it, amazing things can happen. But until we get behind it we'll make ourselves rather uncomfortable, even if we do appear to have everything we could ever dream of.

There is nothing to worry about. One way or another the universe keeps itself in a perfect state of balance. So we don't actually need to worry about the bigger picture, it's always OK. Just look to your place within it, because you can be at one with it or in conflict with it. And that's your choice. It's a choice we all face. Taking a long out breath right now could be the greatest thing that could happen to humanity. It will take a step into the unknown, because none of us have experienced anything but the relentless urge towards expansion. It would of course represent a huge paradigm shift, but at the same time create the space for the most remarkable opening of consciousness the planet has ever seen. If we look to life with our eyes open it will show us, it is always showing us what to do. It shows us what's going on; life speaks to us endlessly. It has been asking us to breathe out for a long time now. Perhaps it is time to listen, because it may not always ask us so politely. If you listen you'll know what you have to do. Somewhere inside we all know what we have to do.

So don't be afraid to look with your eyes open and listen with your heart, and live by what you see and hear, not by what you're told. Listen to it. It's speaking to you through how you feel. Let how you feel be your teacher, let it point you to the way. And wherever you can, try to resist the temptation or tendency to come into conflict with that. Or to not listen to it. Because when you listen and you are with what's going on, it doesn't matter if it's the beginning of the in breath, the middle or the end, the beginning of the out breath, the middle or the end. It is all part of a natural and profoundly intelligent process.

If we are prepared to be surprised, we might find that learning to breathe out is every bit as extraordinary as has been the process of learning to breathe in!

So there we go, this is our invitation. We want to wake up? Life is trying to speak to us. Let's listen to it. Just know that at the end of every out breath comes a new in breath. It is the way of things. When we allow life, as it is, to be our teacher there is never not an opportunity to feel love for what you are a part of.

So where do you need to breathe out? Your heart knows what a relief it would be when you do it. So let go the idea that you've got to be more of anything, and just be. Let go the idea that you have to have more of anything and find a delight in all the things you've already got. And if you don't delight in them, then give them away or share them. Don't be burdened by things that don't add to your life. Let yourself come into the state of balance that is the way of things. To breathe in is to receive, not to take. To breathe out is to give. Find your natural state of balance within the cycle of things and see how much conflict and tension it resolves, and what a relief it could be.

* * *

Key Survival Point For Staying Conscious

How long can you keep breathing in before you feel uncomfortable?

The answer to our problems does not lie in finding ways to take more out, but in exploring what we actually might have to give.

11

Taking A Long Out Breath

I believe that meditation plays an absolutely key role in creating the grounds for positive change within our lives. There is a reason that people have been meditating since the beginning of time. Nobody finds it easy, and it's probably one of the most challenging things a human being can choose to do: to work deeply at unpackaging the hindering layers of conditioning that stop us getting out of life all that we could be getting out of it. I don't mean getting the most out of life as in achieving the most. I mean getting the most enriching experience out of the things that we do, everything that we do, even the ordinary things that normally we wouldn't give a second thought to.

Most of life, probably more than ninety per cent of it, is just a series of ordinary moments. Sure, life itself is extraordinary, but most of the time it is ordinary things that tend to go on.

It's actually a huge relief when you reach a point of not having to always hanker after peak experiences in order to feel satisfied. When you can make each moment a complete moment. Whether it's something as ordinary as making a cup of tea or stepping out and breathing the fresh air at the start of the day. When you pay enough attention and actually completely turn up to what you are doing, almost everything has a moment of serenity to it. That serenity and peace that we are all longing to have in our life arises in the mind when we are fully concentrated on or absorbed in what we are doing. The experience of joy and happiness arises far more often within an experience when we are totally focused upon what we are doing than when we are distracted.

It was to reach these deep states of happiness and contentment that yogis in the past spent long periods of time learning to concentrate deeply within their meditative practice. This is the practice that we call in meditation Samadhi. It means one-pointed and undistracted concentration. In such a state we experience a blissful sense of joy and happiness that surpasses anything we may have experienced with our ordinary mind. It also brings a tremendous sense of relief because in that moment the constant bombardment from our mind ceases. Perhaps what is even more extraordinary about this is that it comes to us within an ordinary moment when nothing particularly amazing is going on; like for example when we are watching our breath.

When our mind is scattered and restless or distracted, we become so crowded out that we don't engage in anything completely enough to actually find it satisfying. Learning to concentrate properly on what we are doing is hard to do and it is meditation that teaches us to concentrate and pay attention deeply. So, creating space and putting less in our lives is probably the most valuable thing we could possibly do. As humanity en masse, creating space and doing less would give the planet an enormous sigh of relief.

Somebody asked me recently why I teach meditation. My initial response was because that was what my teacher had asked me to do when I came to the end of my time with him. But that is not strictly true. I do it because I can really feel so deeply the state of friction that people are living in, and collectively the state of friction humanity is living in, and I genuinely believe that this is hugely relieved when we allow our mind to come back into a more coherent state. And I can feel so deeply the state of friction that the planet is experiencing on account of that friction that humanity is living in.

The real answer is that if we all started to embrace a profound movement towards simplicity in our lives and started to learn to extract the real essence of the experience that we're missing, then we would be of far fewer needs than we currently are. We would be infinitely more satisfied than we currently are. Finding the ordinary things in life to be inherently meaningful would bring a much deeper sense of gratitude than we currently seem to express, and we would move so much more lightly upon this world.

I'm sure everything would breathe a huge sigh of relief if we became less complex and more easily satisfied. We would individually and as a group, as would our planet, all breathe a sigh of relief. So this letting go the things that we're hankering after and overcoming this restlessness that means we're never satisfied to reach the place where we can just be with ourselves and be comfortable and content to just be there is probably the most valuable thing each of us and all of us could do right now. It is this ability that we develop through learning to meditate.

You may have been struggling with the stress of holding a very complex life together, and the idea of profoundly simplifying it may be a million miles away. But through sitting in meditation, learning to just be, without needing to add or take anything from the experience, sooner or later it will probably cross many of your minds; "You know what? I don't need nearly as much as I thought I did". The one thing I see time and time again arising in the minds of those who learn to quiet their minds and become deeply concentrated through long term meditation practice is the joyful enthusiasm for a simpler and less complex life. I can almost feel the planet breathe a sigh of relief each time any of us comes to that place!

Think of all the things that we do, that we occupy ourselves with, that we distract ourselves with - why are we doing them? Are we hoping to find a genuine satisfaction in them or do we all too often do them simply to distract ourselves from how we feel? Have any of them profoundly satisfied us yet? We only do them out of a sense of something lacking.

So why does learning to meditate, something that appears to be almost nothing at all, have the far reaching effect upon us that it does? It is learning to meditate properly, which means developing a deeply concentrated and very calm mind, that brings about a process of repairing the most delicate of mechanisms of our consciousness that allow a simple moment like, for example, standing and looking upon nature at the end of the day, to be a powerfully moving experience. The way we enter totally into a simple experience like that, so it isn't just a matter of looking at something nice but so that it actually moves us deeply, involves the most extraordinarily complex, subtle and delicate mechanism. A mechanism that allows the very currents of life to move through us more freely. It allows this current of life to actually move through us undisturbed by our otherwise restless mind. It is the disturbance to the subtlest qualities of our consciousness that is caused by the constant bombardment of our obsessive and unsatisfied mind. And it is this mechanism that is repaired through meditation. It is the regaining this lost depth to our experience that brings it alive again in a profoundly moving way. Something that at the deepest level all of us recognise we have been missing the moment we discover it again. It is literally like having the lights switched back on, or the poorly tuned medium wave radio suddenly switching over to crystal clear digital stereo.

The damage that we do to ourselves with the constant hankering after distraction and over stimulating of our senses, and by never really engaging properly in what we're doing enough to actually be satisfied by it, fractures these subtle mechanisms of our consciousness that register at such a deep but often unnoticed level. It is these subtle mechanisms that allow us to feel things like appreciative joy, deep gratitude, empathy for each other, compassion and love. And these are the very qualities that add a real sense of meaning to our experience.

All of these experiences register at a deeper than conceptual level. They are all a profound but delicate interaction between the essence of what we are and the experience that we are having. And it takes a coherent state of consciousness in order for those qualities to arise within our experience. It is that delicate part of our operating system that we do such violence to in the way that we live our lives now. We are literally losing our capacity to feel the deepest part of what makes us human.

It is through meditation that we can get back in touch with the very essence of what it is to be human, and the very essence of what it is to be alive and conscious – it is literally reclaiming our consciousness. There isn't anything you could be investing in that would be more valuable in the long run than that and there is no investment that you could possibly make that would cost you less and reward you more.

I'm sure on occasion you'll think, "Is this not a little bit self-indulgent, sitting on my backside meditating?" Yes, perhaps. But when you put your heart into it, and you stick at it, you will start to really, really feel that it's a lot more that you're getting than a little bit of peace and quiet. Almost everybody finds that it takes a significant refinement of character to actually reach a point where the mind becomes profoundly calm and deeply concentrated. It will almost always require the maturing of our capacity for patience, determination and sustained effort, all valuable qualities that will serve us well in the daily life, the very lack of which is often the grounds for dissatisfaction and lack of contentment.

There genuinely is a reason that people have put tremendous amount of effort into learning to meditate. The stillness that I ask my students to tune in to is probably one of the most delicate and subtlest things in the entire universe. The experience of it is one of the most moving experiences that we ever have. Anyone who actually comes to land upon it eventually comes to recognise that that stillness contains a profound intelligence, and coming to that state for most people becomes one of the most moving experiences that they ever have. To be connected to it and to feel our connection to it is often the most alive we will ever feel. So working to develop that connection through the practice of meditation and then, having made it, learning to honour it as what is sacred in our life and taking care of it, is such a wonderful thing to be doing with our life at some level. It almost always adds a greater sense of meaning to life, a sense of meaning that we have felt to be missing. There is only so far we can go with this at a mental level. Beyond that it is necessary to work towards the experience of this through the practice of meditation itself.

Try to tune into what I'm saying from your heart, because it's difficult to convey in a book - it is a knowledge that we reveal within ourself gradually, it comes alive within you as you practice. It is through meditation that we start to glimpse and get a hint of a depth - a more textured, multi-dimensional depth - to our experience than the one we've become used to. Something that is deeper and beyond our initial expectation starts to reveal itself. And the more we open to it the more it has the capacity to inform us in a direct way, in an experiential way, and slowly this learning from experience replaces the tendency to stand upon ideas that we have created in our minds. The more receptive we become to the transformative quantum experience, the more it fundamentally changes us. This is what I am trying to suggest to you - there is a part of you that already knows the truth and it is calling to you to be heard. Meditation is about learning to listen to that call!

This learning to reconnect with and remain in touch with that deepest innate intelligence within us is the journey of awakening. They say that when you pray you talk to God, when you meditate you listen. So when I ask my students to "Rest in the deepest part of your heart," and tune in from there to the stillness in the background, behind things, it's that part of our consciousness that is so sensitive that it hears what's being whispered in the background which is otherwise washing over us the rest of the time, unnoticed. It is when we start to recognise how we do truly feel that we connect to our own innate intelligence, which is always working to bring us out of incoherence and into a state of balance.

When we learn to pay attention to how we are actually feeling we start to recognise the friction that our desire and craving and conflict is producing within us all the time. As our desire and craving fades a sublime inner stillness is revealed to us that has always been there and that is the ground of our very being. We recognise that our true nature is already at peace with itself and that our real needs are very few. Our elaborate needs and desires in truth arise as a compensation for the feeling of lacking that we experience when we are disconnected from our true nature; our true self.

Key Survival Point For Staying Conscious

Meditation teaches us to truly concentrate and pay attention. When we learn to turn up and really be with our experience, we find the magic in even the most ordinary of moments.

Instead of being afraid of a life that has less in it, try to explore what a relief it would be to live a life that not only gave you more time to appreciate the things you do, but meant also that the cost of you being here was significantly less. Feel in your heart what a relief that would be.

12

Meditation: Is There More To It Than We Might Imagine?

There has been a mindfulness explosion in the last few years that has led to a cultural shift in how the mainstream thinks about meditation. But do we really know what mindfulness means and is it alone enough? Mindfulness encourages us to pay attention to what is happening within us and around us. But that attentiveness can arise in a scattered mind and only truly becomes a coherent state when we become concentrated within our experience.

People increasingly recognise the benefits it can have in bringing our mind into an organised and coherent state from one of stress, dysfunction and disorder. While the appearance of mindfulness on the wellbeing radar may well be the first step towards a sea change in our attitudes to consciousness, it will not be the making of us if we are not willing to take stock and accountability of ourselves.

To become a genuine force for positive transformation for both individuals and society at large, it must show the way to a more appropriate way of life. The danger with the current modern secular approach to mindfulness is that by extracting it in isolation from the spiritual context in which meditation has always been taught and the ethical framework that it points towards we may well have missed the wood for the trees.

Mindfulness means attentiveness or awareness. It is the awareness of what is going on within us and around us. It is to pay attention to the experience we are actually having instead of getting lost in the abstract inner world of dialogue, thinking, imagination and fantasy that many of us spend much of our time lost in. Having said that, when we are lost in our inner world, we can be mindful of that too.

As I introduced earlier, the Buddha explained that ignorance is the core root of our suffering. As I said, by ignorance he meant inattentiveness; not seeing things for what they are. The other roots of suffering, greed and anger are in truth merely conditioned by ignorance, or not seeing what is really going on.

Mindfulness can be an important first step in the direction in which we all would like to be heading: less ignorance, less greed and less anger. And certainly we have to start somewhere if we are going to turn around the roller coaster juggernaut that is the direction in which our world appears to be heading.

However, there are two big catches. Firstly, it takes real determination to change in ways that might be inconvenient to us, and that determination itself is a strength of character that we may have to work hard at. Secondly, once our minds become fixed upon a view, position or standpoint and cling to that position, a certain stiffness sets into the mind that is resistant to change itself. This is what we mean by 'narrow mindedness'. As a result we tend to pay attention only up to the point where we aren't too inconvenienced by what we see and so turn away from any inconvenient truths we may come across.

I was recently approached about putting together a mindfulness course in eight bite-sized chunks of 15 to 20 minutes. The problem is that we seem to be looking for a way in which we can extract something of a palliative from these time-tested traditions. We don't seem to have the time that people used to, so we attempt to package it up into the occasional evening class. It almost seems that we are simply looking for something to show us ways to cope better with being where we are. The problem isn't that we aren't coping but that we aren't changing. Not coping is itself a sign that we have reached an unmanageable position and things have to change.

Let's put some perspective on this so we can ask ourselves if we are being realistic. The Buddha himself was born a prince at a time free of strife when the planet was relatively untroubled by our presence upon it. When he looked out upon the world, he saw how prone to suffering we are as humans and made a determination to seek an end to it.

When he went forth to seek the end of suffering, he did so as a prince, with everything in his favour. He was extremely intelligent and physically strong. Even from his relative position of ease he could see that he had to change. He spent six years ardently meditating in search of his goal, and when he found it he spent the rest of his life teaching the path he had taken to others. For over forty years he taught countless others who, like him, freed themselves from the affliction of suffering.

Unlike times past, where even finding a teacher who could guide us often required an act of determination, we have unlimited and almost instant access to thousands of teachings to which we can refer. In most of his teachings the Buddha talks of what he explained as the eight branch process of the refinement of character (The Eightfold Noble Path) that leads in stages to the gradual fading of the roots of suffering.[6] Included in his system was what he called Right Mindfulness. So mindfulness was indeed one of these branches, but it is only one, alongside what he called Right Speech, Right Action, Right Livelihood, Right Effort, Right Concentration, Right Thought and Right View.

These days, as is our tendency with everything, we have looked for a convenient solution to what appears to be our problem. Many of us are feeling overwhelmed, stressed or despondent in our modern lives and mindfulness emerged as the new great white hope. However, we have chosen to develop mindfulness in isolation instead of looking more deeply into what it was that the Buddha was really trying to point out to us. When asked what is the fastest way to free oneself from suffering the Buddha advised that, "He who is of few needs and easy to serve is the closest to being happy".

In his list of the ten qualities that make for less

6   For a more detailed treatment of this subject please see my book, *The Flavour of Liberation, Volume One.*

painful progress in life mindfulness itself does not even appear, possibly because in isolation it does not actually constitute a strength of character. Rather, the Buddha was keen that we look inside to find such qualities as generosity, virtue, patience, honesty and loving kindness. Although they are certainly not the only positive aspects of character that we might develop, the ten qualities that the Buddha suggested are most conducive to a happy and rewarding life are:

1. Generosity
2. Virtue (or harmlessness towards oneself and others)
3. Renunciation (which is the willingness to give up what is not conducive to our welfare)
4. Insight (which is our capacity to understand what is happening to us)
5. Vitality and energy
6. Patience
7. Honesty, including self-honesty (which is a willingness to accept where we are at in life)
8. Determination or resolve
9. Loving kindness towards ourself and others
10. Equanimity (which is the ability to accept things as they are)

Mindfulness alone will prompt us to pay attention to the point that we recognise where we are not coping, and hopefully point us towards some changes that will allow us to do so. But is coping better with where we are a big enough step forward? What of overcoming our unwillingness to change? Do we not think that the other seven branches of the Buddha's path equally had something to show us? Might it be the case that we have run out of convenient solutions and may have to be willing to accept a degree of inconvenience in our efforts to surmount the real challenges we are facing, or free ourselves from real suffering?

It may well have been necessary to dilute the Buddha's teachings in order for them to be palatable for mainstream audiences, but in doing so mindfulness has removed the very essence of what he was really offering us. This is the encouragement to reaffirm basic human ethical principles as the bedrock of the value system that we govern our lives by. What he offered is a road map to take the rite of passage out of the narcissism we become so enwrapped in during our adolescence into the maturity of real adulthood.

We are all humans living on the same planet, and it is not the case that the universe behaves one way for some of us and another way for others. It is a single process that we are all a part of. We are all in this together. So if our lives do feel in a bit of a muddle, the process by which we got there is not personal. The question each one of us needs to ask is whether our challenges will turn out to be our undoing or our making? In the end, this will be our rite of passage and the real test of our character.

Many of us are not willing to take on some honest home truths and get stuck into what is really needed of us. We are all faced with a universal predicament as fellow human beings. Views, dogma and religion have no part in the simple process of self-honesty that is required if we are going to really learn to pay attention to what is going on.

When the Buddha went on his journey it was a rite of passage of the highest order. The journey that truly puts us in touch with ourselves always is. Meditation is not and never has been about watching your breath or your thoughts arise. It's about putting ourselves truly in front of what it is to be alive and entering utterly into it.

The journey up any mountain starts in the foothills. And as a first step, mindfulness is a good place to start out. However, it will not be the making of us if we are not willing to take responsibility for ourselves and find within us the real strength of character the Buddha was pointing at.

There are two things that mark a human being as *extra*-ordinary, and they are generosity and kindness. Not whether we can tap dance around the next person in a conversation, or put on a more elaborate display, or tell stories. Whether we are kind and generous is what marks us as a good person through and through. When we stop asking of life, "What's in it for me?" we start to create a space inside us from which to explore what it is that we might have to give.

* * *

Key Survival Point For Staying Conscious

There is no quick fix to our problems. It will take real depth of character and tenacity to accept, meet and embrace the challenges we face. Real meditation requires qualities like patience, determination, self-honesty and acceptance, all qualities that will help us make the changes that are asked of us now.

Try not to always seek the easiest and quickest solution to your problems. Remember that a band aid does not get rid of the infection that lies beneath.

13

This Life Is So Precious

The extraordinary thing about perspective is that it is always limited by the lens we are looking through. We consider ourselves to be the most intelligent beings on the planet, and at one level we would certainly appear to be. And yet anything that we have thus far managed to create in our most inspired moments pales into insignificance beside the extraordinary creative process that has brought us into being in the first place. A human body? A human brain? A human mind? How often do we stop to reflect on the unfathomably intelligent process that lies behind life itself? How often do we stop to reflect upon how rare this human life actually is?

Right now, with our planet teeming with life and brim full of humanity, it is easy to assume that we would always be here. And yet civilized, complex social humanity has existed for a mere finger snap even in relationship to the relatively short time that life has existed on our planet. Add to that the vastness of space, and the amount of it that appears to be totally incapable of supporting any form of life whatsoever, and we see that our extraordinary planet itself is the rarest of phenomena. And even once the conditions for life actually did appear, it has taken billions of years for the conditions that we are experiencing right now to come about so that we can share the experiences that we have all come to take for granted.

In the recorded history of humanity itself - a finger-snap within a finger-snap, just a few thousand years - much of it has been a hard battle to secure the basic requisites by which we might even be able to enjoy a life that is more than a daily struggle for survival. Finally we are here, having waited aeons for the opportunity to turn up and be a part of this wondrous display that is life. As we argue amongst ourselves about our rights and what we should be entitled to, it is all too easy to forget that it is all over in the blink of an eye. The chances of coming to a fortunate human life are rare beyond imagining; and yet here we are.

The Buddha used to tell a story to illustrate this point. It goes as follows:

"Imagine there was a blind turtle swimming in the vast ocean, and that once every hundred years he raised his head above the water. Imagine then that you threw into that ocean a yoke such as that used to tether an ox, and left it to drift where it may. Greater is the chance of that blind turtle raising his head into that drifting yoke than is the chance of coming to a truly fortunate human life".

Although these odds might sound unfathomable, if you place it up against the appearance of our life bearing planet in the first place, and then within that our appearance at this rare time as fortunate human beings, he might not be far off in his reckoning.

He also identified a number of conditions as the requisites that constitute a fortunate human life, something again he pointed out is most rare. Without them life most easily deteriorates into an incessant struggle. Some of these are:

1. To be born of sound body so as to be able to support oneself.
2. To be born of sound mind so as to be able to recognise basic ethical values and the nature of suffering, its causes and its cessation.
3. To be born in a time free from social strife and upheaval.
4. To not struggle daily to find food and shelter.
5. To be surrounded by favourable companions with whom one does not fight endlessly or struggle in rivalry.

Although I am sure many of you reading this will be facing challenges in your lives, I imagine that many of us are fortunate enough to take most of these conditions for granted. And when we don't have these things we consider it to be most unfortunate. The point here is that it has taken an incalculable amount of time for us to arrive at this extraordinary moment. And yet in the space of a few hundred years we might well, between us, have come close to undoing something that has taken billions of years to come into being. The Buddha used to encourage us with utmost urgency to not waste this rarest of opportunities for it will not come around like this again for a very long time.

So the question we need to be asking ourselves is this. "As the most intelligent creatures on this planet, are we behaving as such?" For nothing else that has appeared here in the whole of the time that life has supported life has ever taken from it more than could be put back. Nor has it *ever* left behind a trace of its presence that had a detrimental impact upon the well-being of other life. In our vast inventiveness we have found ways to take out more than we can put back. But does it mean that we should then choose to do so?

When humanity comes into a time of great fortune there are so many opportunities available to us. One of those opportunities is to explore the fruits of our great fortune. And the challenge is to do it in such a way that it elevates both the quality of our consciousness and our experience and not just our intellect. The challenge is to reach the end of our lives as a more noble being than the one that we were when we were born. This is the challenge that we face when our virtue and our good fortune is still intact enough - to recognise for ourselves what might be appropriate behaviour without having to be told.

How we choose to engage in our life and what we pursue with our life determines where we get to at the end of it. And of course there are so many challenges nudging us away from becoming more conscious. As we become more overwhelmed by the intoxicating level of stimulation we expose ourselves to, it is all too easy to lose sight of the values that lie in the deepest part of our heart. Even when we are an infant we do generally know how we should behave. Somehow we know! And yet when we want something badly enough there is often no end to which we would not go in the pursuit of it. Such is the nature of desire.

When we reject these deeper values in the pursuit of our desires that we think are more important to us, we are in great danger of highly compromising our spiritual wellbeing. It's a very dangerous time as well as an extraordinary time. To live a life so that we might get to the end as conscious or more so than when we arrived is a great challenge right now.

The dangers of undoing ourselves in the pursuit of our desires increases tremendously as our opportunities increase, which is why the Buddha encouraged us to turn our efforts towards our spiritual wellbeing in times of relative ease. It's easy of course to come to the conclusion that the Buddha was somewhat pessimistic, didn't have enough faith in human nature. This certainly isn't the case but he was sincerely concerned for our welfare. And on the other side of this position there are those beings who look upon this world with hope, who see the vision of everything that humanity could be. And they hold that flame, that candle, and they keep it lit, in the hope we could express everything that we're capable of being. In the same way that we are all intelligent enough to understand how easily we could bring ourselves to great suffering, we are imaginative enough to hold in our hearts a vision of everything great that we are truly capable of being.

Those of great faith in the vision of humanity would say to the Buddha, "Hold on, let folk show what it is they could be before you tell them that life is just suffering". And there it is, this profound dialogue, this deep spiritual debate that has gone on since the beginning of time and will always go on. As to whether or not we have it within us to be a testimony to all that we could be, or whether or not for one reason or another, reaching out but failing to get to that place, we bring ourselves to suffering we cannot bear.

(You might like to listen to the accompanying album Brave Souls, Track 3. It's In Your Hand)

In his concern that we would bring ourselves to suffering that we cannot bear, the Buddha discouraged us from being too ostentatious in our aspirations, and told us to commit first and foremost to virtue, and then to the cultivation of our mind, and ultimately to the freeing of ourselves from suffering. Everything else beyond that is a bonus and a gift, but the basic requirement for all of us is that we continue to progress consciously and move in the direction *out* of suffering and not in the direction into suffering.

I've been teaching meditation now for twenty years or so, and in that time I've watched and I've sat with this debate and I've watched students learning meditation. And I'm very much of the mind; "Come on, let's see what we could do with this life that we have! Let's find out what we are truly made of!". But it's a great challenge to live a life well and avoid coming to suffering. So it's important that we come to understand enough of how life actually functions and the potential of our mind to sway us in the wrong direction when we are forgetful. It is very important that the unwholesome tendencies of the mind that bring us to suffering are seen and surmounted sufficiently so that we can pursue this extraordinary adventure and not come to grief whilst doing it.

So what is that point where it is reasonable to say to ourselves, "This extraordinary human life that I have – I'm going to just go out and live it as completely as I can, and see what it is!" Where is that balance point?

Most of us would have been born here with a very high quality of consciousness and good character, and yet we still find it incredibly difficult to keep our head above water, to stay out of trouble. So, we have to be very, very realistic and pragmatic when we are setting our stall out and deciding how we are going to live our lives.

People are coming on my retreats generally a lot younger than I am now and I have to make a decision about which way to guide them. How much insight do I share? What is it necessary to say? What's the right amount? – and how to teach it in a way that we don't live fearfully, that we live courageously and live realistically?

Young people find what the Buddha is pointing at very challenging. It has huge implications when we realise it for the first time. It's a big thing when you see and you realise actually how responsible for yourself you are, because then you have to take on that responsibility. When we don't, we really feel the weight of not taking that on responsibly.

Right now, we find ourselves in a delicate position where we are not experiencing abject suffering but still capable of coming to it; where the extraordinary opportunities of a fortunate human life are still wide open to us. This is an extraordinary place to be. But we need to recognise how rare and how fortunate that position is; that we still have it in our hands to determine our own welfare and where we go from here. It is so important that we take responsibility and take the steps to avoid coming to unnecessary suffering. Because it is much harder to free oneself from suffering than it is to get into it. If you have sufficient faith in your own integrity and you are willing to completely and utterly stand by that and not compromise it, no matter how many things push you, you'll still need to know what the boundaries are if you are to safeguard your own welfare.

We can't have everything. We just can't. Each of us has to work this out for ourselves. And then, while you still have your destiny in your own hands, while it is not dictated to you by another what you should be doing, while you have freedom of choice and the support that you need, then don't wait thinking it's something you're going to do in the future. Do it now! Whether it's to go and live your life 100% and show it can be done without harming others and without consuming the planet. Or whether you seek to free yourself totally from suffering now and in the future, and show equally that that too can be done. Do one of those things, but don't do neither of them, please, not with this life, not this very precious one. Don't do neither because you couldn't commit to either, and then be one of those people who at the end bitterly regrets not having done it, because a chance like this won't come around again for a very, very long time.

While you have this life, you have the chance to make a strong determination to live your life impeccably and make it extraordinary, and work very, very, very hard at what you have to do. A life of ease comes when we have done what needed to be done. But it doesn't come before that. Anything short is complacency. So let's not over-indulge now, because it brings us in real terms so little reward. Do what you came here to do, one way or the other!

THERE IS a place the other side of which we're free from suffering, where we will not come to grief we cannot bear. That is the place that we all long to get to. And if we are honest we all know that we only ever get there by paying attention, living considerately and doing what we have to do. It is in our hands. The choices we make now will determine whether we reach that shore where storms no longer rage and the wind is cooling to the soul.

* * *

Key Survival Point For Staying Conscious

Stop and reflect upon how long you may have waited for the precious opportunity that this life offers you. Don't waste it. It's just a short time and you won't get another one like this for a very long time!!!

*(You might like to listen to the accompanying album
Brave Souls, Track 1. How Great Was Our Longing
& Track 11. It's Just A Brief Time)*

14

Our Responsibility As Guardians Of The Planet

The Buddha talked of the wheel of life, in which those of good fortune tend to consume that good fortune until it is gone and then find themselves having to toil endlessly to recover it again. Those who lack good fortune have to toil endlessly to accumulate good fortune, only to consume it without renewing it as soon as they find themselves no longer struggling.

And so we migrate endlessly from times of good fortune to times of misfortune, on account of failing to recognise the conditions by which such good fortune comes to us. Or, by failing to use our current good fortune as an opportunity to sow the seeds for our continued good fortune in the future by doing meritorious deeds that benefit others in the world around us. Regardless of whether we hold the view that life continues after death the way the Buddha describes, or whether we believe that everything ends with our final out breath, we are all part of a continuous cycle of life that started with our ancestors and continues with our offspring. It may not be us who inherits our own good fortune or lack of it, but it will certainly be our children. If we look back over our ancestral timeline I am sure that all of us will see that we have migrated many times from good fortune to misfortune and back again.

If we look out across the world everywhere we can see four categories of beings:

- fortunate people whose good fortune is increasing
- fortunate people whose good fortune is decreasing
- misfortunate people whose misfortune is decreasing
- misfortunate people whose misfortune is increasing.

Each of us will fall into one or other of these categories.

From this perspective we can look at our life pragmatically and look for ways to maintain a balance so we aren't using more of our good fortune than we are creating or being unrealistic in our expectations and demands. It is a little bit like managing our bank account. If we always withdraw and never deposit, sooner or later we run on overdraft. Once that happens our life starts to get significantly more challenging. If we max our overdraft and our credit dries up we are really in trouble. Well, life works in very much the same way. Certainly some of us come into this life with more 'good fortune' in the bank than others. But it is important to remember that good fortune is not just a reflection of our financial situation. Many wealthy individuals see their life fall apart at some point on account of various non-financial conditions. Our mental and physical health are, of course, obvious examples of such conditions, as is the quality of our companionship with others, the way people respond to us and so on.

It is more often the case that one of good fortune sees such good fortune as an opportunity to take more out of life at a personal level, rather than seeing it as an opportunity to give more back. If we remember what it has cost in terms of the energy and resources that have been consumed to keep us here, we can see that those of us who are fortunate cost far more to have here than those who are less so. It seems that the more fortunate we are the more we lean on our deposit accounts. We're cashing in a tremendous amount of good fortune in order to be here. The question is, "Are we sowing the grounds for such good fortune in the future?"

So right now it is a time of extraordinary good fortune, but a time at which it is costing more to have us here than can be sustained. What do I mean by that? The amount of material resource that it takes to keep every human being on the planet right now - including the people that have hardly got anything - as an aggregate, the global ecological footprint is about 1.6 times the total renewable resources that the planet is capable of producing. So all of us, i.e. humanity as a group, are using up every year 1.6 times what the planet can offer. It is clear that we are using up too much resource too quickly.

As I mentioned at the beginning of the book, in 1970 the World Wildlife Fund calculated the point at which in that year we had consumed as much renewable resource as the planet was capable of providing. From that moment on, we live on overdraft. This year (2016) the WWF calculated that we had used all of the planet's renewable resources by August 8th, which meant that for almost 5 months we lived on resources that would not be replenished.[7] The fact that the planet had been able to sustain us at the level we were consuming it until 1970 is a testimony to its extraordinary bounty.

Had we stopped at that moment to recognise just how much we *are* given freely to support our human aspirations, and chosen at that point to put a limit to our levels of consumption, we would be having very different discussions today about our vision for the future of humanity and our planet.

I ran a simple test with my mother a while back using a basic series of parameters to tally up the total resource cost of her being here.[8] She lives alone in a moderate three bedroom house, and has a comfortable but not opulent lifestyle. When all was added up, it turned out that she was using 7 times more resource to keep her show on the road than the level set out by the WWF as sustainable. Now her personal consumption levels were greatly elevated because she lives alone and runs a household for just a single person, which means there is no spreading or sharing of any of her consumption. But the shocking realisation was that while humanity as a whole is using 1.6 planet's worth of resources every year, we in the relatively well-provided for parts of Western society are consuming at levels vastly above what is sustainable.

---

7   http://www.overshootday.org/
8   http://calculator.bioregional.com/lstep01.php

Now of course, much of our consumption is offset by the large numbers of people still consuming below the sustainable level, but we perhaps need to start asking ourselves whether the expectations we have about how we might lead our lives are reasonable.

When I ran a survey amongst my students on a year long programme who sought to investigate ways of giving back, we quickly came to the realisation that the way our lives are currently geared just isn't set up or aligned towards contributing to or even significantly reducing our consumption levels, because of the level of demands already upon us just to, 'keep our show on the road'. Even where there was a great willingness to do so, we found that there is a point beyond which it is very difficult to go, for one seeking to lead a significantly less consumptive way of life. I was quite disheartened at first to see just how much inertia there was behind the direction of travel that we have set ourselves upon and so I went away for a while and reflected deeply on what might be done.

I came back to the notion of cycles, and even the simple rhythm of breath itself. I remembered back to the time I first watched *Al Gore's* film *An Inconvenient Truth* and the graph he showed explaining the increase in the rate of consumption of carbon based fuels at that time. I remember thinking, this has got to give! The graph showed that in the last 70 years we have consumed more than we consumed in the whole of history before that![9] What was so staggering to me at the time was, if it is so blatantly

9   http://web.ncf.ca/jim/ref/inconvenientTruth/ (the plate with time code: 00:23:53)

obvious that things could not go on the way they are, how did we manage to convince ourselves that it was OK to continue in the same direction without real change?

Through my reflection it became so clear. The problem is that we are simply so used to breathing in. We are so used to having our whole life and our vision of it geared around the idea that life is about expansion and increase, or that the future needs to have *more* in it to make it better, that we have no viable vision of what life would look like if we all started to breathe out. And yet, somewhere inside we are all desperately waiting for the opportunity to do so. We are literally dying to breathe out. The problem is that we have no reference points for what an 'out breath' life would look like. The question we need to start asking ourselves is, "*How* can we realign our vision and aspirations for life around the notion of the long out breath instead of the in breath?"

Perhaps we need to ask not just: "Are we using the planet's resources more quickly that they can be regenerated?" But, "Are we using our good fortune more quickly than we are generating it?" We are obviously taking out more from the planet than we are giving back, but is that equating to a greater sense of happiness, enjoyment, meaning and contentedness in our lives? The planet itself and the world we are born into is a boundlessly creative source, and it produces no end of things for us.

It's not the case that we can't take *anything* out. There is so much rich bounty for us to appreciate and enjoy without us becoming a burden. There is so much that we are gifted and the planet will continue to keep giving to us if we take care of it. So it is of course reasonable for us to enjoy it. But there is a point beyond which we are clearly taking out more than is reasonable. And once we start to do that we are actually drawing on our stock of good fortune, and depleting the supportive energy behind our lives.

So if we start to look at the life we live as relatively fortunate humans in developed societies (i.e if we take out all the people living subsistence lives, who are using very little to be here), we see we are using anything between 3 and 7 times the resource that the planet can afford to give. Which means we're consuming between 3 to 7 lifetimes of supportive conditions in a single lifetime. It means what we're taking out in one life is what could have supported 7 fortunate lives. If we are going to take that much out, we must surely try to make it count – that we appreciate it deeply and that we give back as wholeheartedly as we possibly can while we have the rare opportunity to do so.

When you play your trump card, in any game, you should make sure to play it wisely. A life as fortunate as we enjoy in the West is like playing a trump card – we won't get it often so we should not let it slip by. Please think about how you can use it wisely for your own growth and for the benefit of as many others as possible. Please reflect upon how you might live it as helpfully and considerately as you possibly can, because that's how you flourish in the long run - that's how human beings come to flourish and not struggle. When we stop asking what's in it for me and instead reflect upon what we have to give, we will see over time that there is so much in it for all of us.

A proliferation of suffering is always a reflection of a degeneration of consciousness. An increase in wellbeing and happiness is always a reflection of the refinement of consciousness. These are basic universal laws. It is how energy moves. The seed of a bitter lemon will never bring forth sweet fruit no matter how much you put water on it. But a mango seed will always bring forth sweet fruit because that is its nature. If we want to see the good fortune of the human life and the human condition improve we all must find ways of contributing to the pot that is supporting it. We must all find ways to sow sweet seeds that in time will bring forth sweet fruit. The love and the care, the humility and the gratitude, the appreciation, the compassion, the generosity and the kindness that it would take to create a truly beautiful world, this is what we must find within our own hearts. Each of us can find this so that we can become the architects of such a world. We create such a world by making choices and taking action and not just by praying and hoping that it's going to just turn out OK. Why would we expect things to change or turn around if it is still driven by greed, lust or selfishness?

We see that if we want a beautiful world we have to make the choices that will create and bring such a world into being, and we must look to see what we could do to contribute. I would suggest that thinking seriously about what we can give back while we have a life as fortunate as this is a good way to play our trump card. It is a great danger to spend such a life merely pursuing our fancies.

It is by being consumed with the pursuit of our personal desires that we mark the transition from good fortune to misfortune. I am sure none of us want to have to go through what that entails. So let's be diligent, attentive and courageous about the way in which we set our stall out in this life. Because in our hands is not only the future of those who are going to come after us, but our own future too. The choices we make now will determine our future. We are experiencing the effect of past choices made throughout history and what we choose now will create the history to come. The way the world plays out is governed by this and no amount of learning to bend it to our will is going to provide a refuge if our good fortune wanes and the support to our lives runs out.

And that is the tragic irony around the predicament we find ourselves in. It is costing us and the planet more and more every year to keep our show on the road, and yet more and more of us, as each year goes by, are finding that our lives feel less and less meaningful. If we really were having the time of our lives as we consume our way through the rich bounty that comes our way, then perhaps we could possibly stand upon the 'dine well, for tomorrow we die' argument, even if it shows itself to be lacking in concern for those who will follow us on this journey. But the truth is, we aren't as happy as we would like to be. We aren't having 'the time of our lives'. Not only are we living in an unrealistic way, but we aren't actually even enjoying it that much.[10]

---

10   There were 50 million prescriptions for anti-depressants issued last year in the UK - the highest ever number and 7.5% up on the year before. mind.org.uk

How many of you would embrace the idea of a simpler, less complex life with less in it if you thought there was a way to get there? According to a survey we recently ran over 80% of you do. Just prior to going to print with this book, we ran a survey asking some basic questions about how people are feeling about the quality of their lives. Some interesting statistics that emerged from it were:

- 80% of people felt a need to improve their overall state of mental wellbeing and general state of mind.
- 80% felt the need for more simplicity and space in their lives.
- 83% of people feel there is a need to change the way we live to safeguard the world we pass on to the next generation.

So whatever else we think we've got to prove, the one thing we really have to prove is whether we can learn to live here in a balanced way. Now that's a real challenge if you are looking for one! But if you are driven by the perceived need to prove something else, to get the nod or the thumbs up, or to be seen by others, you might want to think about letting that go. You aren't here to be seen or to get the thumbs up. The only thumbs up that are really worth working for now will come when we have shown, each one of us, that we can bring our lives back into balance and live in a way that safeguards the future for those to come.

* * *

Key Survival Point For Staying Conscious

This has been a staggeringly beautiful planet for billions of years. It is in our hands as to whether our children get to witness it as that. If we do not choose to start using less now, it is a certainty that they won't.

15

The Never Ending Cycle

So it is clear when we just think about it that the choices we make define our life. The effect of past choices don't just go away, even if in the future we decide we want something different to what we chose at some point in the past. Take partnerships for example. Many people end up in relationships and start families with a partner who later they decide they do not wish to be with. Or, just as often, they meet someone else that they feel they want to be with more and on account of that desire they seek to leave behind the family they once chose to start. So even rationally and logically we can look and see that we are bound by our actions at one level or another because the consequences of them play out over time. And so being attentive to how we feel before, during and after we make choices and take actions that might define our lives in some way is extremely important.

But let us now try and see if we can get a sense of how we are bound not just by our actions but by the volition that prompts them. By volition I mean desire, will or intention. It is this volitional aspect or wilful aspect of consciousness that the Buddha called karma. Volition is the aspect of consciousness that prompts us to act. As he said "It is volition that is karma; having willed I act" i.e it is the volition or intention behind our actions that is karma.

Every time the mind arises it produces a charge within our nervous system. The quality of that charge determines how we feel. For example, when we are prompted to act by anger, the aversion that arises in our mind produces heat in the body. That heat itself is an unpleasant experience, and when it becomes excessive, it alone can feel unpleasant enough to lock us into a state of aversion. Once we react with anger to any given experience, when we encounter such an experience again in the future we already carry the tendency to react with aversion or anger again. It is the feeling that arises within us when we experience something that prompts us to react in any given way.

This is the process by which our behaviour becomes conditioned. These conditioned responses are what we are referring to when we talk about 'karmic tendencies'. The karmic energy that we carry is the charge accumulated by our habitual tendencies and reactions from the past. In this way our present is conditioned by the past, and the future is conditioned by the present. In such a way unwholesome states such as anger, greed or craving can become accumulated habitual tendencies within us to the point that even when we tell ourselves that we should not be so angry or so greedy, we continue to react in such a way. Our responses become hardwired into us, or conditioned into us. The process of freeing ourselves from such conditioning so that the mind is no longer driven by greed, craving or aversion is the very operation that our meditation performs upon us over time if we learn to do it in an appropriate way.[11]

I do not wish to get into a lengthy discussion on karma here as I am aware that for many this is a contentious subject. It is far too often assumed that karma is the result of our actions. What it actually refers to is the volition or intention that is prompting them.[12] I simply wish here to illustrate how the volition that drives us to act is the charge that we hold on to at an energetic level going forward once the action itself has come to pass. This charge works upon us to condition the way we respond, act and react to the things that happen in our life. We are bound to our past choices not just because of the implications they have in our life and what it means our life is made up of day to day, but because they condition the quality of our life and our experience of it by conditioning our reactions to life.

We can see this at work all around us. There are countless people who have everything one would think might make for a happy and rewarding life and yet they remain dissatisfied or unhappy within themselves. This is because the quality of their mind reaches a point where they are no longer able to extract the pleasure and happiness from the pleasurable experiences when they do arise. What is more, we often notice that those who are surrounded by the most fortunate of circumstances are the least able to forbear hardship and challenges when they come. The flip side of course is that many people with what we might consider to be very challenging lives,

---

11   The meditative practice that transforms our unwholesome habitual tendencies and conditioning into wholesome ones is the practice that we call Vipassana or Insight meditation.

12   Please refer to *The Flavour of Liberation, Volumes 1 & 3*, Burgs

full of hardship, manage to find a peace and contentment within themselves.

So when we look closely we can see that our mind in any moment is colouring the experience of what happens, depending upon how it is habitually inclined to react. Let's take for example our ability to concentrate, or its opposite, our tendency towards restlessness. As I have already discussed, as our ability to concentrate upon what we do deepens, so we start to find our experiences increasingly rewarding. So when our mind is composed and able to concentrate and sustain its attention, we are capable of finding immense pleasure in the simplest of experiences, like beholding the beauty in nature or appreciating a great work of art or even preparing a meal. But when our mind is scattered and restless, even the things that normally would be pleasurable pass us by almost unnoticed because our mind is always hankering after or fretting about something that is not actually happening.

We can see that in extreme cases this could reach a point where, blessed with everything we could possibly imagine, we find ourselves so distracted that we find no joy in anything. On the opposite side of the scale we can also see those whose minds are composed and balanced enough so that even when there is not much going their way, they are capable of finding great meaning and satisfaction. We can all see examples of where this is the case in the world around us and perhaps also in ourselves.

The truth of this was so clearly illustrated to me during my time living in Java when I was running my clothing business years ago. I met my first teacher Merta Ada a few years previously and would regularly accompany him as his assistant whenever he ran meditation retreats around Indonesia. At that time I was travelling often between Java and Bali. Every day I used to ride my motorbike to the factory in Bandung, and every day I would pass the same traffic lights and more often than not be held up at the junction. And every day there was a legless man at this junction who was propped up on a wooden box playing his harmonica and busking for change. This same wooden box was where at night he took shelter and slept. I never once passed that point without seeing him smiling joyfully. He would always wave to me as there were few westerners in the city at that time. In spite of the extreme hardship he faced in his life, his eyes were bright and creased not from vexation but from smiling and joy. I had just started learning to meditate and at the time was still finding it uncomfortable to sit for an hour cross-legged. Each time I waited for the lights to change I would reflect on whether I would be able to find such a positive attitude if ever I found myself as challenged as this. I very much doubted that I could.

At that time I would often fly down to meet with Merta Ada to accompany him on retreat, and on one occasion I remember him telling me an extraordinary story about a billionaire businessman who had visited him that week having had a stroke. It was 1997 and the monetary crisis had just hit Indonesia. The Indonesia Rupiah had fallen from 2500 to the dollar to 15000 at its worst moment. This man came into the clinic telling of his woes. When Merta Ada asked him what his problem was he told the following story:

"Oh, it is a disaster. I had 700 million US dollars in offshore banks around the world. Then one day a friend of mine told me that here in Indonesia the banks were offering a 20% interest rate. So I moved all my money back into the country a few months ago and now the monetary crisis has come. I have lost so much money I cannot believe it. I will never get it back in all my life. The stress has been so great, I am sure it was the cause of my stroke".

After hearing of his woes, Merta Ada asked him, "So how much money do you have now?"

"Now I have only 100 million dollars left."

"And do you still have a house?"

"Yes, I still have my house in Beverly Hills and in Zurich and my villa here in Bali."

"Well," replied Merta Ada. "I would consider you to be a very lucky man. Imagine if everyone who had less than that to their name became so stressed about their misfortune that they had a stroke. I would be a very busy man."

When I heard this story I remembered the legless busker in Bandung. I realised that in truth, in spite of his challenges, he was far better equipped mentally to both find joy in his life and face challenges when they come.

This brings me on to such an important point. It is one of the single most important realisations we can come to in our quest for happiness and contentment:

"My life and the quality of it is far more

conditioned by the quality of my mind than it is by what happens to me".

Now when you started reading this book that might have sounded like quite a bold statement, but are we getting to the point where we can start to really see that that could well be true? Because that has such huge implications when we roll it out into our life and re-evaluate the choices that we make.

For example, we might have come to the conclusion that this wide array of things that I've set out - my hopes, my dreams, my ambitions, my aspirations - would need to be fulfilled for me to find my life complete. But all these things together may have made our life inordinately complicated. It may have made us most vexing to other people because of the nuisance we make of ourselves in the pursuit of all our needs and desires. It also made us extremely costly to have here on the planet while we pursue all of these things.

So look at what happens, not just to us but to our world, when we realise that that sense of meaning, satisfaction and completeness doesn't hinge upon any of that vast array of things I've decided to go and pursue or seek to acquire. It hinges solely upon whether I can make friends with myself right now in this un-extraordinary moment. Because 95% of our life will be made up of ordinary moments. In those ordinary moments I am a nuisance and inconvenience to no one, and it's costing so little to have me here.

For many of us this represents a paradigm shift in our approach to life. When we embody this understanding it brings about such a profound transformation. It's unrecognisable from the trail of chaos we can create around us and the energy it requires from all quarters to uphold our elaborate orchestrations and carryings on pursuing our desires. Compared to when we go about our business quietly, unassumingly, almost unnoticed, going our way peacefully and happily, finding the joy in simple things.

Now if you take one person and they make that transformation – that's a little bit less vexing for the world and everything in it. If you take a handful of people who make that transformation – there's a little bit of a sigh of relief. But take lots of people who make that transformation and withdraw that disturbance and all the energy that is bent one way or another to make things go their way. Now you are experiencing a profound sigh of relief from the whole planet in every possible direction.

So the simplest thing you could possibly imagine doing, sitting still, meditating or just being and doing nothing, might well go on to have the most profound effect that you could possibly have upon the world, not because of what you're going to do, but because of what you're *not* going to feel the need to do any more. And that doesn't mean that you're going to go and spend your entire life in a room looking at the wall. It means that you're going to find enough joy in the things that are already in front of you to find your life worthwhile, meaningful and enriching without having to continuously take more out.

There's a story I would like to tell.

"Once upon a time, high above the earth in the shimmering realms of the heavens, lived various classes of radiant beings, each one of a higher level of consciousness than the next. The first condition for any being to enter into even the most ordinary of heavenly realms is the single baseline quality of virtue - not cleverness or inventiveness, but virtue. And then beyond these realms are other realms of increasing radiance as beings and their worlds become more and more coherent, until they become sublime in their consciousness.

Now what happens in those lower realms of heaven, where beings' minds are simply pure, is that they just delight in the beauty of the things around them. That delight alone is enough to keep them in awe of and in love with life. So when they come to know of a world such as ours, goodness me how they long for the opportunity to stand upon the earth like this and look upon the things we see every day, displayed in all its beauty in nature. These beings are breathtaken and mesmerised by the beauty of the nature that surrounds us that daily we take for granted.

And then above them are those beings whose consciousness becomes more and more refined, who on account of their imagination start to become more and more creative, and start to make music the sound of which you have never imagined, beautiful sounds to move you in the depths of your soul. And they create visual displays within their highly imaginative minds that are truly intoxicating beyond description.

And then, as their consciousness becomes

more and more refined, they become more and more absorbed in their own creations, and they stop looking at what is displayed everywhere and effortlessly, by creation itself, but become fixated instead on their own displays. And finally they become so intoxicated with their own creations that in creating them, they consume the very ground that their world stands upon, until there comes a time when in their creativity they consume everything, and their world becomes a wasteland."

In this story that highest expression of consciousness folds in upon itself because it forgets the very ground of its own being, becoming so intoxicated in the idea of itself that it forgets where it came from and it loses its connection to everything that once it delighted in. Well, this becomes a cycle upon which the universe turns and unfolds time after time, endlessly. The wheel of creation itself coming into being and passing away without end.

Perhaps we can see some of this process at work in our world today?

It's not until we can find enough satisfaction, meaning and contentment in just being that we stop consuming the ground upon which our life stands. For all their creativeness those beings in this story could not create anything as extraordinary as what they already were; and nor can we, try as we might. We already are the highest expression of the creative principle. We have just lost sight of that as we became intoxicated with our own idea of ourselves.

This beautiful world and the beings in it are

the infinite expression of the creative process itself. That is what life *is*. That is what we might call divine! And this is what you wake up to every single day, if we could only learn once again to pay enough attention to it.

There is nothing, nothing, not a single thing that we have created or ever will that will come close to being as extraordinary, intoxicating or imaginative in its creativity as the natural expression of life itself. Your iPad? Your iPhone 6? Your Xbox One? Your Oculus Rift VR headset? Or this world and everything in it? Come on! What are we thinking!

Just this summer I spent time with a friend who had his daughter visit him in Ibiza. Her cousin came to stay for a day. Having grown up together they had not seen each other for a whole year. They spent the entire day sitting in opposite corners of the sitting room, staring into their phones, and hardly spoke a word to each other. They were not interested in going out on the boat, to the beach, or even going out socially in the evening. Their virtual world was clearly already more appealing than genuine human contact and connection. When I asked her about it, she just said, "But you don't understand. This is how we do things now". She was convinced it was a step forward to the way the older generation used to do it! I have to say, I beg to differ.

The things we have turned towards in our quest of satisfaction, seeking...what? What are we seeking? What are we hoping for? What are we thinking we're going to get in our endless expression of ourselves? It's already expressed perfectly within you every moment.

For so long life on this planet has expressed itself perfectly in its vast, imaginative and creative display, with not a hair out of place. As I mentioned at the beginning of this book, over this time life has perfectly recycled everything it created and didn't deplete itself one tiny little bit. And you have been part of that since you took your first breath. What is it that you think you need to add that could possibly make it better than that?

We don't know how to live unsheltered and unclothed - fair enough. So I think that food and shelter is a reasonable basic requirement. Of course it is! And some degree of things to occupy ourselves with, and company and companionship, that is a wonderful addition too. But the rest of it? The rest of all the stuff we pick up and cast away with the blinking of an eye? Are we really deriving any genuine satisfaction from all this stuff we are consuming? And the crazy thing is we're not even delighting in being the creators ourselves any more, we're simply delighting in the creation of others. Whoever made your iPhone, your iPad, your car? I am sure you didn't get the satisfaction of making it yourself.

No-one's suggesting that we are not going to enjoy ourselves and explore life. But I am suggesting that we could reach a place where we needed to take much less out of it than we thought or than we are currently inclined to do. Let's just imagine for a moment: let's put a little pile together on one side of all the things it's taken to get us to where we are right now in our life. Then let's put in another pile on the other side everything we have contributed to the pot we draw upon in the search for satisfaction. How is our balance account looking? In credit or debit? How many lifetimes do we think we would have to work to create that much ourself by way of giving it back? So let's not take it all for granted, and let's not consume our vast accumulation of good fortune as if it was going to last forever. Make it last forever! Because it can. Until we appeared here it did last forever.

When you can sit quietly and find a simple joy in just being here in an ordinary moment, then you will instinctively start to tread a little lighter, and it won't be noisy inside you, and it won't be crowded out, and it won't reach the point where we feel suffocated by our lives. Finding a joy in a moment such as that is the gift that meditation brings us, if we are prepared to put the time and effort in to turning around our mind; to turn around our unbearable restlessness and craving for more into the ability to really concentrate and the contentment that brings to us in any moment.

I haven't yet met a single person who made peace with themselves and then chose a more complicated, elaborate life. I haven't. So surely this elaborate and complicated life cannot be the resolution, or an expression of being at peace with ourselves, or happy? We all want to be happy. We all want to be happy! We're all longing for it. The problem is we have forgotten where to look.

It is important to understand that when you do find happiness you *will* tread lightly – you just will.

And that lightness will translate back into the very core of your being as a lightness of spirit, and all the weight that we are exhausted from carrying around will begin to drop off us. Now that is such a wonderful thought, isn't it?

* * *

Key Survival Point For Staying Conscious

The quality of our life is utterly conditioned by the quality of our mind. As we become more disconnected we find our experiences less satisfying. This leads to an endless pursuit of pleasure as a replacement for the happiness and sense of contentment we are lacking.

(You might like to listen to the accompanying album Brave Souls, Track 6. The Joy Of Simplicity & Track 5. Turn Up For It)

16

There's Only Love
And Not Knowing It

Looking for solutions to the challenges that we face as humanity without adding some kind of spiritual context to it feels to me to be akin to seeing those challenges merely in terms of whether we can survive and feed ourselves, when we should be delighting in life at every level. There is little doubt that in our inventiveness we will find ways to produce food more efficiently, and quite possibly we may soon learn to tap the vast resources of energy that lie in the quantum vacuum and use them to fuel our lives in the absence of the rapidly depleting carbon based reserves.

However, have we considered that it may not be as simple as whether we survive, but the manner in which we do it? We are now capable of keeping ourselves alive for longer than ever, but equally, degenerative chronic diseases are proliferating at unprecedented levels. We are surviving, but is the quality of our lives improving? All of my mothers' grandparents died peacefully in their sleep, slipping away with a quiet out breath as life reached its term and the body was worn out. Only two of my grandparents were that fortunate. These days I rarely hear of someone dying of natural causes. Almost everyone I am asked to support through the dying process finds this final rite of passage to be a tremendous struggle, involving a protracted period of sickness and a medicated final stage.

We remain conscious for longer but the quality of that consciousness is being highly compromised. It costs us more than ever to be here in material terms, but are we deriving more joy from the experience? I hope by now, at this stage in the book, you will agree that we need to change. Not just because it is becoming glaringly obvious that the planet is creaking under the stress we have put it under, but because we are likewise creaking.

Surely there are some fundamentals that need to be intact for life to be a meaningful, rewarding and enriching experience? We do not have to look far to see how easily it can become little more than a struggle to survive in the face of abject misery. We in our modern developed societies may not face a daily struggle simply to survive. But we are all capable of recognising that the quality of our life ebbs and flows. And that it would appear that we far more frequently find ourselves feeling that something is lacking, than we experience a deep sense of meaning and joy at being alive. While we have gradually eroded our connection to the idea that life itself is sacred, we have fought tirelessly to uphold our own position here with a diminishing recourse to the impact that that is having upon life in general; and by that I mean *all* life. Not only has the life of so many of the other creatures that we share this planet with suffered on our account, but the quality and integrity of our own life as humans has likewise started to degenerate at levels we may only now be starting to recognise.

Life *isn't* easy. It is a profound and mysterious thing, and it is delicate. For it to flourish so that it can express itself in its fullest potential within us, we perhaps need to honour it as deeply sacred once again.

It is interesting that one of the ways by which we judge our human consciousness as superior to that of other animals is in terms of the ability that we have developed to bend the natural order to our will. To bend the natural order to create a more convenient and comfortable life for ourselves. The danger of this of course is that in doing so it has brought us into such dramatic conflict with that natural order, to the point where we now are the only species alive on the planet, with the possible exception of those animals that we have domesticated, that is not able to live directly in nature.

I remember some years ago reading a report telling of an increase in the activity of solar flares on the surface of the sun, and the increased risk that a large such flare might produce so much electromagnetic radiation that our electrical grid might go down and with it all of the internet. I sat for a while reflecting on this when I finished reading the article and realised in that moment every other living being on the planet would net gain from such an event while we would struggle desperately to keep our lives on track. It was so clear to me in that moment just how separated we humans have become from all of the rest of life.

Our lives are held together by our ability to

continue to bend the natural order to our will, while every other living being survives only for as long as it is able to live in accordance with that natural order. While everything else lives by and depends upon the creative intelligence of nature itself, we live and depend upon the world that *we have created*. It really does seem that we have become those beings who in their intoxication with their own creations have lost their connection to the creative intelligence itself. That to me is the single most compelling indicator that we are living in a way that is not just unsustainable but untenable. And even more importantly, exhausting. At every level it is exhausting. We are exhausting ourselves and exhausting the very planet our lives stand upon.

One of the biggest complaints I hear from people is that they just don't have time and they cannot afford to simplify their lives. But a simpler life is both more affordable and affords us more time! It is an argument that just doesn't stand up. Are we simply afraid of the space that might be left behind when we do start to breathe out?

The second complaint I hear at the suggestion that a simplified life might be the doorway to more happiness is that people imagine that their lives would be profoundly boring and uninteresting if they did let some of the things in it go and start to breathe out and simplify.

What I have to say to such a claim is this. We haven't yet satisfied ourselves in the pursuit of our desires. What makes us think that our satisfaction and contentment is going to come from adding something new to the mix? It is not. Our satisfaction, our peace, our contentment and our sense of meaning is going to come when we discover something in our lives that is already there, that has always been there, and that in our endless distraction with our own creative pursuits, we have failed to recognise.

If we are no longer amazed and in awe of life, it is not because it isn't amazing and awesome. It is because we have become too numb in our over-stimulated but distracted state to recognise what is going on here. One of the things that happens time and time again when people learn to meditate, and hence learn to concentrate and pay more attention to what is going on, is that they rediscover a sense of awe and wonder that we may have had in childhood, but that we so easily lose as we progress along the path of our lives.

As I have said many times already, there is an intelligence that rests in the background behind our lives that is so profound and so moving, but perhaps even more important even than that, is that when we do find ourselves coming into contact with it, whether by meditation or some other means, invariably we come back from the experience convinced, even knowing deeply that it is so full of love. And isn't love one of the things we all yearn for more than anything else? One of the human heart's deepest longings is to come to know, experience and feel love.

I recently saw a wonderful cartoon of a young boy gazing in wonder up at the stars in the night sky. The caption read, "The Universe only appears to be made of matter...but secretly it is made of love". Now you might think that sounds a little dippy but how much wonder does that young boy still feel when he gazes at the stars that so many of us have stopped feeling because we are too distracted or too numb to completely turn up?

And if we are feeling depleted and exhausted, where do we think our energy actually comes from? The vitality that supports our life is not produced by the food that we eat. Although that gives us our metabolic energy that drives all the mechanical processes within our physical body, vitality itself is something deeper and more fundamental than just metabolic processes. Like all living things we rely on consciousness to produce vitality within us. As I have said, when consciousness stops arising within an organism, all vital signs cease. Our vital energy is a reflection of our connectedness to the vast living field of energy that all things exist within. This universal field of conscious living energy is the basic ground to our being and it is infinite in its potential. It fuels all life tirelessly for as long as that life remains plugged into it. Almost all spiritual traditions refer to it in one way or another as the basis of all life.

Today science is also starting to posit the notion that there is an intelligent field of energy that is alive and conscious that sits behind the appearance of things, and that it appears to be limitless in its energy. After centuries of trying to fathom the material universe in the absence of factoring in the role that consciousness plays in the process, even science is on the brink of having to acknowledge the possibility, if not yet the fact, that we are living in a conscious intelligent universe, and that for all our creative ingenuity we humans are far from the most intelligent part of it.

Science some years ago began to acknowledge that the energy contained in the apparently empty space between matter contains vastly more energy than does matter itself. The empty space is what contains the energy. Some scientists have calculated that there may be as much as 10x1040 times more energy in the empty space than there is in all the matter that appears within the universe. As the physicist Richard P. Feynman once described in attempting to give some idea of the magnitude, "The energy in a single cubic meter of space is enough to boil all the oceans of the world".

When we touch this field of intelligence within our meditation, we come to know that not only is it still and profoundly peaceful beyond words, but it is not empty, but alive with a sublime consciousness that rests effortlessly within itself and is free of any sense of conflict. From this boundless field of pure potential all things come into being effortlessly. And what is more, this source from which everything arises is in no way depleted by that which arises out of it. This is the energy we are tapping into when our mind becomes still at night when we sleep, or when our mind stops for a while in a state of concentrated meditation. It replenishes us in that moment that our mind stops, and it is deeply nourishing, restorative and healing. But the experience of connecting to it is also profoundly moving and in an instant cuts off any sense of complacency and leaves us once again in awe of life.

It is the losing of our connection to what lies in that stillness between the coming and going of things that has created in us such an unbearable sense of lacking. And that yearning for something we haven't got has driven us to uncover every stone we could possibly uncover and go down every rabbit hole we could find in the search for something in the material world that is going to satisfy. But it never in truth comes close to satisfying. We are always left with that yearning for something else, and so our endless pursuits go on and on until we have consumed everything there is to consume. Meanwhile, all the time and everywhere, that tireless and boundless energy continues to support us in spite of everything we manage to do to cut ourselves off from it.

The creative power of this pure intelligence that underpins our life is so profound and so moving that to just reduce it down either into a series of scientific formulas or to come to the spiritual conclusion that it is just a process of 'dependently arising phenomena' is to lose sight of the fact that it is still a miracle beyond our comprehension.

Jesus called it "The peace that passeth all understanding". The Buddha, while referring to the boundless or unconditioned state as the ground of all things, acknowledged when asked about it, "I have cast my mind back over beginning-less time and I cannot see the original coming into being of things". Both of these great masters admitted that there is a mystery in the background behind our lives that is beyond our concrete understanding, and yet it is the coming into contact with it that leaves us in no doubt that life is both sacred and meaningful and intelligent beyond words. The point for both of them, and for all of us, is not to vex ourselves trying to fully understand it, but to come to the experience, or at least trust that it is or even might be there.

And *that* I believe is the heart essence of the whole problem we face. Why have we become so obsessed with our perceived need to understand life, when actually what we long for is just to be in love with it? When we stop taking life for granted and remember how delicate and sacred it truly is it will not fail to astound us in its beauty. That is what leads us to acknowledge it as sacred and to honour it as such. In such a moment we begin to sense the love that rests in the stillness from which everything is effortlessly arising and passing away, even if, as Jesus acknowledged, that love is beyond our understanding. The rich tapestry and display before us in life is surely an expression of love; surely it could not be that beautiful if it wasn't? I cannot find any other way to explain how it got to be as extraordinary as it is.

When in my meditation my mind becomes clear and coherent, if then I concentrate deeply and calmly or with love and I put my mind into a sugar substance, for example, and I let crystals form as that sugar dries out and I look at them under the microscope, they are so exquisitely beautiful, in the way that a snowflake is naturally beautiful. But if I don't put loving kindness to that substance, if I just put a miserable old grumpy feeling-a-bit-sorry-for-myself kind of mind into those sugar crystals, they do not form beautiful structures. An experiment similar to this was carried out multiple times by the Japanese scientist *Masaru Emoto*, documented beautifully in his book, *The Hidden Messages of Water*, looking at the effect of consciousness on the way ice crystals form.

Have you ever seen an ugly snowflake? Since nature is always and everywhere beautiful, I do not posit the fact that it is just a mundane type of consciousness that brings all of this into being. I posit the fact that it is a profoundly intelligent and loving consciousness that underpins our lives. When I look at the world and everything in it, what I see is just love and not knowing it, and that is all there is everywhere. Life as an expression of love, and life as an expression of not knowing that love. It is the pain that we experience when we do not know love that drives us to do all the other things that cause us such suffering. There is no judgement. Not knowing love is only worthy of compassion. There is no other way that you could possibly look upon another being that doesn't know love.

So perhaps we might reflect upon that: life everywhere is a reflection of either love or not knowing it, and that's all you'll see everywhere. When you look out at nature you will see that love expressed all around you. When you see people confused, don't judge them, they might just not know that love yet, or they might simply have forgotten it. So try to learn to love them to death anyway, whether you can make sense of them or not, and I think in that way the world would be a happier place for it.

* * *

Key Survival Point For Staying Conscious

"The Universe only appears to be made of

matter...but secretly it is made of love". So go and discover that for yourself. It is not knowing this love that is the cause for all the suffering we bring ourselves and others to.

(You might like to listen to the accompanying album Brave Souls, Track 4. Dance Your Own Way)

Part Three:

A Give Back Generation

17

Giving Rise To An
Age of Regeneration

"May your heart always be joyful.
May your song always be sung."
                                    - Bob Dylan

So where does all this lead us? Where do we go from here and what are we going to do?

The Buddha spoke of two scenarios in which consciousness flourishes and suffering diminishes. In one scenario, humanity as a whole gradually loses its moral compass and the age of degeneration proliferates. In such a time, virtue and consciousness survive only in remote places amongst a handful of people who remove themselves from the influences towards degeneration and build their lives and communities around virtue, harmlessness and balance.

In the other scenario, humanity as a whole rediscovers its moral compass and takes stock of its tremendous impact and responsibility upon the earth. Rising to the challenge they face, humans embrace their role as guardians of the whole and, appreciating deeply their good fortune, start to contribute to the welfare of all, cherishing it as highly as they cherish themselves.

In such a time they do not head to mountain caves and remote forests to free themselves from suffering. As families, communities and social groups, they flourish together, living in balance with their world and in alignment with the intelligence that their life truly stands upon.

We are the generation who will determine which of these two conditions comes to pass. It is our time, and this is our rite of passage. This book has pointed towards how we might realign with a more natural intelligence behind life. So what do we actually learn when we start to align to this intelligence and recognise how life is really functioning?

As we have seen, all life has a cycle of growth and a cycle of decay or fermentation. Consciousness as a driving force behind life equally has a cycle of expansion and contraction. The vital force behind consciousness that supports the growth and flourishing of life is love, kindness and the exuberance that is born of the simple joy of being alive, when it is expressing itself coherently. When consciousness degenerates towards greed, selfishness and ill will, the decay or fermentation cycle sets in. Life has a force to it, and when that force is positive and loving by nature, life expresses itself in no end of sublime and beautiful ways. When that conscious force degenerates, life degenerates with it.

Over time we come to see that when the deeds of people are driven by greed, selfishness, aversion and pride, consciousness degenerates and with it the world we live in. It is not possible for it to be otherwise. However much humans are able to bend the appearance of things to their will, life will always express itself as a reflection of the driving force behind it. No amount of imagination or effort to control life wilfully can hide us from the gradual loss of the integrity of life that sets in as consciousness degenerates.

When the deeds of people are driven by kindness, generosity and loving regard for self and others, it is a certainty that over time consciousness flourishes and the world is regenerated with it. It is not possible for it to be otherwise. However much suffering we witness in the world around us, when we learn to see our suffering and challenges as our invitation to evolve rather than allow them to be our excuse for undoing ourselves, this tangled knot of suffering begins to untangle itself.

The natural order maintains itself. It is not bettered by our presence here, nor does it depend upon us. However, it does depend upon our not bending it so out of shape that it can no longer support us. We are utterly dependent upon the natural order and in every way life is made better by living in line with it.

Every day we take out more than we put in, our soul withers in some small way. In time it becomes barren and destitute and loses its sense of purpose. It forgets how to love. Every day we put in more than we take out, the soul shines a little more brightly.

I am often asked, how does one who is suffering improve their condition? Often it is not possible to improve our condition in the here and now, but what we can do is improve the conditions for what we will meet in the future. This is done through living in a beneficial and not detrimental way. The way you improve your condition is by contributing more than you take out so that at the end of your life your contribution account is greater than when you arrived. The Buddha talked of those deeds that bring genuine benefit as our merit. The merit that it takes to come to such a fortunate human life as this is unfathomable. To renew our field of merit in this life so that we leave here as fortunate as we arrived is to live a successful life. This good fortune is not reflected in our stock of material possessions for none of those will carry on with us when we go. Our good fortune is reflected in the quality of our mind and our capacity to find joy and happiness in life regardless of what is in front of us. There are countless beings who, born with the most extraordinary good fortune, end their lives not having renewed the field of merit that supported such a life and leave struggling endlessly to find a peace at the end of their lives as they attempt desperately to hang on to what they are about to be separated from. It is a great shame whenever a life so full of potential and good fortune ends in suffering such as that.

I was walking up the drive the other day and I looked out across the field at some sheep. Now it is all too easy to see these sheep as stupid animals that are here to provide meat and wool. However, to have the wool taken off your back on a regular basis so that someone else can be warm while you are in the freezing cold, goodness me, that's an act of generosity and sacrifice.

To have your young child taken away and not to complain about it, this is an act of patience and forbearance. To produce milk for the sustenance of another, that is an act of merit. To be killed so that your body can be a support for another, that is an act of great sacrifice and merit. So the sheep might not have arrived on this earth with much merit, but hopefully they go out with more than they came. Certainly it is the case that they give more than they take out.

It reminds me of an ancient fable in which a great king, on the occasion of an annual feast, approached the goat that is to be sacrificed. Looking down upon the animal, he noticed a tear running down its face. Moved by this, the king says to the goat, "Oh, you poor creature. I am sorry for what I am about to do." To which the goat replied, "But sir, I am not crying for myself, for my suffering is about to end."

The world doesn't ask much of us and it gives boundlessly. It only needs us to not be a burden. It doesn't ask for more than that. To live in such a way that our presence here is neither a burden to the planet or those around us is to succeed in life. In this way do we secure our own welfare and show the way for those to come. In such a way we play a part in the regeneration of our world and the healing of the wounds we have inflicted in the past. It will be a long time before an opportunity such as this comes our way again. It will never come our way again if we do not take care of it now.

When we reflect upon our life, we should perhaps not look only to the things we consider to be our achievements, but perhaps start to ask ourself if our life has been a field of merit or benefit in any way? There is more than an ecological benefit that might come from removing from our lives the unnecessary elaborations, letting go what is not necessary and exploring what delight there may be in simplicity.

The direction in which our world is moving is the greatest signpost there is as to how we will fare moving forward. Our life here and how we lead it has always been the doorway to our future, so reflect hard on these things, for there is far too much at stake to just ignore them. We cannot assume that everything will just work out fine simply because we hope it will. If change is needed, be willing to change. If you need to change, change yourself, without expecting it of the next person. They may well be waiting just to see your example.

Learn to stop and be still for long enough to look upon this precious earth that we live in and gaze upon it in wonder and honour it as sacred. If you find this hard or if you can't feel this, if you don't know this to be true, then get back out into nature and keep doing it until it slaps you awake with a sense of awe and wonder.

Open your heart with real humility and grace, spend some time reflecting deeply upon what it is to come into being at all, until any tendency to take it for granted, and any sense of entitlement, is gone. And then find ways to allow your heart to be touched by the divine principle that is at work everywhere, sustaining you and all life.

Learn to say thank you from the deepest part of your heart until you really deeply mean it. The real intelligence behind our life is the only refuge we ever really have, so find your way of getting in touch with it. Make a deep reflection on how precious is this opportunity that you have now.

You will find your own connection to this boundlessly exquisite and loving intelligence within your own heart, when you step out and look at the majesty of nature and feel it bringing things into being, endlessly, everywhere, despite everything that we might have put in the way. Look around you. Everywhere on this planet that life can come into being, it comes into being. On a rock, on the bark of a tree, even in the most barren of places, the smallest things come into existence. This creative principle, this power of life is the divine at work, and we are all but cut off from it. Let go the pride that prompts you to compare yourself to others, so that you can see that your real needs are few, and far more easily provided for than you might have thought, and then try to live your life as harmlessly as you can.

Virtue

If you take just one nugget from all of these pages, it should be that the way to flourish in life is to commit wholeheartedly to living considerately, or what we could call virtuously. As a meditation teacher, I implore my students to put their commitment to virtue and the right effort towards refinement of character at the top of the list of priorities in this life, even above all worldly or spiritual aspirations.

If you are inspired by the accounts you may read of the sublime states of bliss and peace that can be attained through meditation, know that none of them will ever be as pleasing as living a life that is free from regret and remorse. And that comes only from our commitment to virtue and harmlessness and the way in which we choose to conduct ourselves.

What did the Buddha mean when he talked about virtue? Well, there are what we call five basic precepts which he identified as being necessary to maintain a mind that is free from regret in a householder. These five precepts constitute the basic commitment for one who aspires to live harmlessly.

Below I briefly outline some recommendations that are loosely derived from the five precepts. These are not intended to be a prescriptive set of commandments, rather things to reflect on and potentially aspire to and continuously work towards.

1. Do good things that are of benefit whenever you can, and if possible make your livelihood something that is of a beneficial service. Avoid doing things that have a harmful effect on others. If you cannot be of service in your livelihood, then make sure it is not harmful.

Most importantly, do not take what is not given to you, or seek to acquire what is not rightfully due to you through deceit.

2. Do not take life and wherever possible do not harm another being deliberately or through carelessness. Seek to help all of those who can be helped by you in any way. If you are able, try to be a vegetarian or at least show restraint with regards to the eating of meat. When you do eat meat, try to reflect upon its source and not eat what has been inhumanely produced. And when you do, offer thanks to the one who has provided for you.

3. Be honest and trustworthy so that your word stands for something. Do not speak of those you know in ways that would cause others to think negatively of them. Do not brag and boast about your achievements or speak in ways that seeks undue reverence from others. Try to show modesty in your actions and words.

4. Do not indulge yourself in sexual misconduct or in ways that would cause you to become driven by lust to the point where you become consumed by it.

5. Avoid such intoxication that leads to such a loss of your mindfulness that you would do things or make decisions that you might later regret, or harm others in unrecognised ways.

These are the basic guidelines for the well-faring of all of us. It is not rocket science, and every spiritual or religious teaching worth its salt, since the beginning of time, will have implored others to do just this. Find a delight, if you can, in aligning your life towards harmlessness and benefit and away from the harming of yourself or others, be that physically, mentally or spiritually.

When I finished my meditation training in Burma and left the monastery I was in, I spent some years studying healing and traditional medicine with a Burmese healer. His medicines were most powerful and over the years I have seen extraordinary results come to those how took them. But every time he would give this medicine to anyone he would ask them first to commit to those five precepts of virtuous conduct. It was a request he made of everyone before he gave them medicine.

When I finished my training with him he asked me to share his medicines with my own students of meditation if they needed it. One day I asked him why he insisted on asking his patients to commit to the precepts and whether it was inappropriate to take the medicine without doing so.

To this he replied, "The medicine is merely for keeping strong and healthy the body. The precepts are to keep them free from suffering".

* * *

Key Survival Point For Staying Conscious

To live in such a way that our presence here is

not a burden to the planet or those around us is to succeed in life. It is in this way that we secure our own welfare and show the way for those to come. Think about how you might reduce the burden you place upon the planet and increase what you contribute to it.

(You might like to listen to the accompanying album Brave Souls, Track 1. How Great Was Our Longing)

18

Sowing The
Seeds Of Change

Spending our lives wondering what we should be doing with ourselves, or finding ourselves doing something that isn't meaningful to us, is a real shame, for anyone who isn't struggling daily to survive.

We *do* have a debt of gratitude to pay back. Although we should not carry this like a weight around our necks, we should embrace the notion that it has come to us to safeguard the future wellbeing of not just us humans, but all life upon this planet. The Buddha used to say that we could never repay our debt of gratitude to our mother whose sacrifices to bring us into this life are great indeed. It is likely too that we will never repay our debt of gratitude to the precious earth that holds us and sustains us. In many traditions it is the earth itself that is called Mother. Perhaps it is time that we started to see it as such and find the kind of respect that a mother is due. It is good to take time to reflect, even daily if we can, upon how unbelievably fortunate we are. We might also stop to reflect upon what it actually takes to keep each one of us alive for the time that we are here, and realise that is such an extraordinary gift. And no matter what it is that you achieve in your life through the pursuit of your desires, you won't at the end of it reflect as gladly upon your time here as you will if you have given of yourself in some way that brings joy and happiness or eases the suffering of others.

As I said earlier, kindness and generosity are the true mark of an extraordinary being. All the other things that we're battling with, all the inner demons, they are all put to bed when we just find generosity of spirit and start to give of ourself. Not because we think we have to, but because we deeply feel so grateful and we know that we have so much to give.

If we all were, from this moment, to make the decision to start giving of ourselves in any way we can, when we reach the end of our time and we look back at what we had contributed, it could be enormous. We have the choice to do that, and to weave such an attitude into our lives somehow. And we're all wondering somewhere inside, "What can I do that's going to make my life count?"

Find your way of giving back, or of being of service to others. Not necessarily in an extraordinary way that's going to change the world. You're not going to change the world. But you could contribute and be some small part of the change that is really being longed for at a very deep level, not just in our hearts but by the whole planet.

Each of us, when our needs become fewer, could make a tremendous difference to those whose needs might genuinely be greater than ours. And while we do it, let us give our precious planet an opportunity to rest and reorganise itself and catch its breath while we take our long out breath...

Think about how you could tread a little lighter. Think about it until you see that it is not a sacrifice to do so but a relief. It always comes as a relief to know that we tread a little lighter, for so many reasons. Not just because you have to struggle less to uphold your life, but because more quickly you reach that place where you've got something to give back.

There is no swifter and more direct resolution to the myriad problems and sense of discontent that humanity en masse is experiencing right now than learning to put back, to give back at a group level, to this planet that we're on and to those who are less fortunate than us. It's in our hands. The direction in which this goes is in our hands. Ours alone.

Nothing else on this planet impacts it in a negative way. Everything else on the planet has found a way to be here without degenerating the integrity of the whole. We are considered to be the most intelligent creatures ever to have appeared on this earth, and yet if we are not careful our stay here could end up lasting only a few thousand years. It is a finger snap in the wheel of time. Even the dinosaurs managed to succeed for 180 million years with brains far less developed than ours. The choices we make and the way we choose to live our lives from now on will determine where we are in fifty years' time, when our children look back and look out at the world that we've left them.

Let's look intelligently at what it means to not be struggling for our survival and see that it's our calling to give of ourselves. I don't know how long you might spend trying to work out your place in the world amongst your friends. And how to make your parents happy and feel good about yourself and decide whether you should do this or that and where you should go and all that kind of thing ... but try to stop it. It doesn't matter. None of it matters. The mark of you when you come to the end of your life will not be the display that you have put on. It will be what you gave of yourself for the benefit of others.

Some part of your time you most definitely should use for the deep enjoyment and appreciation of this life. The things that you cherish, honour them, give them time, don't crowd your life out so the things you really want to do deeply you don't get round to. And part of your life try and give of yourself, whatever way you can. And then you will have a deeply rewarding life that is of great benefit. It is for your wellbeing and the wellbeing of others. If your personal needs and ambitions remain great, you may well find that you spend your entire life in the pursuit of them and fail both to have the time to appreciate them when they do come or to give back in some way for the benefit of others. In such a case, regardless of what you may appear to achieve in the material field you will end your life less fortunate than you arrived. And that would be a great shame.

So try to simplify your life enough so that your needs are met with part of your time so that you can dance and give with the rest of it joyfully. And don't worry if the person next to you doesn't quite understand what you've decided to do. Just get on quietly, be willing to go unnoticed just doing your thing and one day, in some way, you'll start to make a difference. And people will look at you and they won't go, "What on earth does he think he's doing?" They'll look at you and go, "Hmmm. Something's going on there." When you put your heart into that, your heart will shine and others will want a bit of that too. And when they see why your heart's shining you might be the prompt for them to change.

So don't wait until you have to change; until you have no choice. Choose to change. Choose, joyfully! Because when you act decisively through choice, so much energy moves in support of what you do. When you are forced to do something reluctantly there is so much friction behind what you're doing. Choose now, at this time when your good fortune is at its most, instead of looking for more good fortune and hope it's going to get better... it doesn't get better than this, folks. It just doesn't get better than this. This is the point at which we start giving back. There's enough there for you, and if you haven't got enough yet, share with each other so that it goes round. So you can work together as groups, so our group needs are less. Then you really can make a difference.

If in some of you right now there are lights going on and you are thinking, "Yeah, I get it. I get it!" Then go and do those things that you're thinking about doing now. Don't in one year's time look back and regret that you still haven't started. If you have been feeling in a bit of a muddle make sure you *aren't* still feeling that this time next year. Get on with it! Look back in a year's time with your eyes blazing, with your plan well and truly under way, with the foundations being laid.

I know it's hard. It's hard to change the momentum behind our lives, it's hard. But it can be done. You can deeply change the things that make you tick, profoundly change the things that you want to get out of bed for, so that they are genuinely for your wellbeing and for the wellbeing of others.

Take some time out if that's what you need. If you're exhausted and you've been pulling your hair out trying to keep your show on the road give yourself a proper break, time to connect back to a deeper current of your life and let it really start to work through you and express itself through you. Because there's lots of things that are distracting us right now. You need rectitude and tenacity to walk a straight line, and it's worth investing the time in finding that, so that when you give of yourself, you're giving from a cup that's full; so that it is not sacrifice, but a gift, so that it is just generosity, just kindness.

Nothing withers your soul more than knowing that you didn't contribute. Nothing makes your soul shine more brightly than the knowledge that you are finding meaning in your life and benefiting others. Sow these seeds in your mind and bring them right to the forefront. Don't worry about how you thought you had to live your life. Think inventively about how you might.

* * *

Key Survival Point For Staying Conscious

Simplify your life enough so that your needs might be more easily met. Give up whatever you do not truly need, as joyfully as you can, for the wellbeing of others. Do not wait until you have to change or until you have no choice. Choose to change, and choose, joyfully!

19

A Give Back Generation - Mighty Oaks From Acorns Come

"Yesterday I was clever, so I wanted to change the world. Today I am wise, so I am changing myself."

- Rumi

There will be no shortage of people who say that the suggestions I am making are totally unrealistic. But before doing that, perhaps stop and ask if it is not simply the case that they are inconvenient. What if we find out in just a few years from now that life like this just can't go on? Then what? What if it were to turn out that our lives have been totally unrealistic and that by failing to see that we have undone ourselves? How hard it is to change will in the end only be a reflection of how far out of balance we have allowed ourselves to get.

Sometimes the signs of good fortune may not be what they appear, and we may not always recognise the opportunities that come our way. It is a sign of the degeneration of consciousness that those of good fortune suffer as much, or even more, than those with little. One who needs only food, water, shelter and fuel in order to sleep at peace at night, and works daily in the beauty of nature to gather those few needs, may well be suffering less than one with many needs who is never satisfied. Such a person often finds that they spend almost all of their time in the pursuit of those needs with little or no time left in which to appreciate the fruits of their labour.

Imagine for a moment that there was something you wanted very badly. What would you be willing to do to get it? Would you be willing to harm yourself or others in the pursuit of it? If you wanted it badly enough, perhaps there would be no limit to what we would do to acquire it. This is the point at which life begins to degenerate.

It is all too easy to come to the conclusion that our individual influence here upon the earth is so small and insignificant that it doesn't matter what we do, or that there is no point of trying to change things. However, the point is not to try to transform the world but to transform ourselves. That is our contribution to our welfare and the welfare of others; to not be a burden to them in our time here. Our world will only begin to change when we start to change, each of us, from the inside. We should seek to get to the place where what drives us, inspires us and prompts us to act, think and live, is gradually driven by wholly positive aspirations.

The highest of all aspirations is the longing for the genuine wellbeing of ourselves and others. In short, love. Love is the longing for the happiness of another, and when it is stripped of all selfish desire, pride and sense of entitlement, it expresses itself unconditionally, not favouring one being over another. And it doesn't need anything back in exchange.

Throughout this book I have spoken of the two principles which govern the evolution of consciousness out of a state of suffering into one in which it is free from suffering. I have tried to point to how we might live and delight in being alive, without being oppressed by mental affliction and without undoing our planet in the process of celebrating what it is to be alive.

So again these two golden rules are:

- Try not to take out more than we put in
- Be totally unwilling to harm ourselves or others in the pursuit of our desires or while we delight in this life.

It is easier said than done, of course, but in effect, both of these principles are an expression of love.

In truth, when we strip life down to its basic principles, everything we will see, and all the beings we will encounter, as I said, are either an expression of love or not knowing it. In the heart of each and every one is a longing to witness, to behold, what this life is capable of being. It is our hearts' deepest longing, for we all know inside what it could be. We long for that more than anything we have ever longed for, and if we have forgotten this, it is only because of dust in our eyes. We may still struggle to overcome our greed, selfish desire, anger and aversion, but our true nature is love and always has been love.

When we sow an acorn in the ground, the vision of it as a mighty oak may well be far from view. But as soon as it is sown, the possibility of it becoming that is born. A forest emerges gradually over a long period of time, yet it is always the result of seeds sown just expressing their true nature.

We exhaust ourselves looking for a model that will define a brighter future for our children, that will bring this world into a state of sustainable balance and peace. The resolution to our problems does not lie in the hands of our political thinkers and economic strategists. It lies in the heart of each and every one of us. The world around us is always a reflection of the consciousness of those upon it.

When we sow the seed of love deeply in our hearts once more and water it so that it shines forth, slowly our world will change. Weeds struggle to gain purchase in a forest of mighty oaks but once the oaks are cut, wild growth proliferates. Anger and greed struggles to find purchase in a heart that pours forth a loving regard for all beings equally.

There once was a time, in the distant past, where love was the creative principle behind our lives rather than desire. Sometime in the future this will be the case again. It is the way of things, the cycle of things. Every storm that blows one day comes to an end. When it does and the waters become still and calm again, they become a mirror which clearly reflects anything held before it.

Our mind is like water. When you calm it and allow it to be still, it will likewise become a mirror. And when you do that, it also will reflect everything perfectly that it beholds. When it does, you will see for yourself that your true nature, and the true nature of everything, is love.

In the most tempestuous of storms, it might appear to be anything but that. However, always and everywhere, the same truth holds sway. When things are left to settle naturally, they express themselves beautifully. The more disturbed they get, the more distorted.

So let's try to start our own revolution, each and every one of us, not by shouting out for change, not by expecting it, but by becoming it. Positive change starts with a revolution in the mind. The change we are longing for will be brought about by kindness and generosity and pouring that forth boundlessly in all directions to every being that comes our way.

That light of love in your heart may well start out only as the faintest of glows but it is the flame that marks us as human. If you want to make it blaze brightly, you will need to tend to it and put fuel upon it so that it might get a heart to it. At that point you will recognise that it is true; your needs *are* few and they will already have been met. So take the time to sow the seed of love in your heart, and make generosity and kindness the basis of your life.

Even when you are angry or depressed, there is always a way that you can do something for others, to give in some way that adds a little light to the world. When you do this daily so that it becomes your habit, gradually you will lose sight of yourself and your need to be seen, and in that quiet moment your heart will be open and you will know love.

Sometime in the future, a time will come when, as you draw your last breath, you will look out upon the world and see that a whole forest of mighty oaks has grown up where once you placed little acorns. But what is more, that light that you shone upon those around you will have touched them in unspoken ways, so that they got to planting acorns too.

If then, as that last breath leaves your body, you can find it within your heart to say thank you to the extraordinary life that you have been a part of, you will fare well. And beyond your wildest dreams you will see how extraordinary this life truly actually is.

Don't wait for the world to change, don't wait to be told what to do, don't even wait for the next guy...Start right now! Take that seed of love and sow it in your own heart with a simple reflection, "Thank you, thank you, thank you".

Write it on a piece of paper, stick it on your mirror and every morning as you wake up and every night as you go to sleep, make this reflection. Hold it in your heart until your flame of love starts to blaze. For when it does, you will not need anyone else to show you the way. You will know what it is you have to do.

So good luck to each and every one of you. Keep at it and never give up. And one day our children will dance together in a world of mighty oak forests.

* * *

Key Survival Point For Staying Conscious

It may well be that you do not see the seeds you sow come to fruit, but rest in the knowledge that others will.

Remember the two golden rules that safeguard our true welfare for the future: "Try not to take out more from life than we put in, and be totally unwilling to harm ourselves or others in the pursuit of our desires". From little acorns come mighty oaks...get out there and start planting seeds.

(You might like to listen to the accompanying album Brave Souls, Track 3. It's In Your Hand)

Epilogue

If you have found this book hard to read, I apologise. I know it is bitter medicine. But it seems it is a bitter pill we need to take. It may well be that you have felt deeply sad, or even shed a tear along the way. If that is the case, then it means you are still in touch with your heart. That is never a bad thing. It is OK to feel sad, perhaps even important, because what we are doing to ourselves and our world is sad, but it doesn't need to be that way. The saddest thing of all is that we don't realise that it is happening.

That tear you shed is a sign that you are getting in touch with how it feels. Stay with that feeling, be with it for as long as it takes to end whatever numbness you may be feeling. Even if it is uncomfortable, find the courage to be with it because it is that feeling that will tell you what you have to do. That feeling will always show you the way home whenever you are lost. So whatever it is you have to do to end that numbness you should do it...because goodness me, this world needs people like you to find that love which is the true ground of who you are, and go and share it with the next guy.

Summary Of Key Survival Points
For Staying Conscious

Ch1. Life's Deep Mystery

Learn not to ignore things but to look as honestly as you can at life and what is going on around you. Try to stand courageously in the face of whatever you see rather than pretend it is not happening.

Ch2. The Momentum For Positive Change

Explore the idea that we are not just facing an environmental and economic crisis, but a spiritual and moral one. Until our basic attitudes to life and what it means to be a human changes, we are unlikely to find solutions to the worldly challenges facing us.

Ch3. Reconnecting To What Really Matters

When we disconnect from our heart and its real aspirations, hopes and dreams, we are often left with a feeling that life lacks meaning and is empty. This is one of the reasons we end up pursuing our desires in the hope that they will give us the sense of meaning we have lost. Ask yourself from your heart, "What do I really want out of life?" The answer may not be what you initially would think.

Ch4. Does Flourishing Mean We Always Need More?

Is it really enough to just cope? Ask yourself, "How much of my life has been a struggle? How much of my life have I spent just coping? How much of my life have I felt that I am actually flourishing?"

Reflect upon how this might change if you simplified your life. Instead of trying to put as many things as you can into it, try to bring more quality to the things that you do.

Ch5. Are We As Conscious As We Think We Are?

There is far more to consciousness than intelligence and our ability to think. Feeling is the real essence of our experience. We often use our thinking minds to compensate for the fact that we are numb to the actual experiences we are having. When we learn to feel again (both the pleasant and the unpleasant), we rediscover the real depth of our experience. This is how we really become more conscious.

Ch6. Reclaiming The Heart

There is more intelligence in the heart than there is in the brain. It is through the heart that we reconnect to the real intelligence behind life itself, something that may have confused us at a mental level for a long time. The love that lies in the background of our lives reveals itself gradually to our heart and not our mind, as we learn to feel deeply again.

Do whatever it is you have to do to overcome whatever numbness you are feeling, however hard it might be.

Ch7. Life Is Consciousness, Consciousness Is Life

The universe is conscious and alive and sacred by its very nature. It is our failure to recognise this that has allowed us to feel justified in the way in which we exploit it. When we learn to recognise that the whole universe is conscious, we recognise also that we are accountable for our actions. Learning to see that all life is sacred brings us back to a place of deep respect for it.

Ch8. The Age Of Individuality; When Consciousness Turns In On Itself

When we stop comparing ourselves to others and fixating on our need to be seen, we recognise that our real needs are far fewer than we think. The more elaborate is our idea of ourself, the less easily we find contentment and happiness. Try to notice just how much your idea of yourself imposes itself on what you do, and see how much freer you would be to dance with life, once you start to let the ego go.

Ch9. The Cost Of Convenience

Ask yourself whether all the conveniences we have added to our lives have actually improved the satisfaction we get out of it. How much has all of this convenience contributed to the numbness we are feeling? Reflect upon what might have been the real cost of convenience.

Ch10. The Long Out Breath

How long can you keep breathing in before you feel uncomfortable? The answer to our problems does not lie in finding ways to take more out, but in exploring what we actually might have to give.

Ch11. Taking A Long Out Breath

Meditation teaches us to truly concentrate and pay attention. When we learn to turn up and really be with our experience, we find the magic in even the most ordinary of moments.

Instead of being afraid of a life that has less in it, try to explore what a relief it would be to live a life that not only gave you more time to appreciate the things you do, but meant also that the cost of you being here was significantly less. Feel in your heart what a relief that would be.

Ch12. Meditation: Is There More To It Than We Might Imagine?

There is no quick fix to our problems. It will take real depth of character and tenacity to accept, meet and embrace the challenges we face. Real meditation requires qualities like patience, determination, self-honesty and acceptance, all qualities that will help us make the changes that are asked of us now.

Try not to always seek the easiest and quickest solution to your problems. Remember that a band aid does not get rid of the infection that lies beneath.

Ch13. This Life Is So Precious

Stop and reflect upon how long you may have waited for the precious opportunity that this life offers you. Don't waste it. It's just a short time and you won't get another one like this for a very long time!!!

Ch14. Our Responsibility As Guardians Of The Planet

This has been a staggeringly beautiful planet for billions of years. It is in our hands as to whether our children get to witness it as that. If we do not choose to start using less now, it is a certainty that they won't.

Ch15. The Never Ending Cycle

The quality of our life is utterly conditioned by the quality of our mind. As we become more disconnected we find our experiences less satisfying. This leads to an endless pursuit of pleasure as a replacement for the happiness and sense of contentment we are lacking.

Ch16. There's Only Love And Not Knowing It

"The Universe only appears to be made of matter...but secretly it is made of love". So go and discover that for yourself. It is not knowing this love that is the cause for all the suffering we bring ourselves and others to.

Ch17. Giving Rise To An Age of Regeneration

To live in such a way that our presence here is not a burden to the planet or those around us is to succeed in life. It is in this way that we secure our own welfare and show the way for those to come. Think about how you might reduce the burden you place upon the planet and increase what you contribute to it.

Ch18. Sowing the Seeds Of Change

Simplify your life enough so that your needs might be more easily met. Give up whatever you do not truly need, as joyfully as you can, for the well-being of others. Do not wait until you have to change or until you have no choice. Choose to change, and choose, joyfully!

Ch19. Mighty Oaks From Acorns Come

It may well be that you do not see the seeds you sow come to fruit, but rest in the knowledge that others will. Remember the two golden rules that safeguard our true welfare for the future: try not to take out more from life than we put in and be totally unwilling to harm ourselves or others in the pursuit of our desires. From little acorns come mighty oaks…get out there and start planting seeds.

GUIDELINES ON
SAFE USAGE FOR TECHNOLOGY

Although the term 'Digital Detox' has been around for more than a decade, it has more recently been making an appearance in the media recently. I think any efforts we might make to safeguard the quality of our consciousness in the absence of making a genuine effort to reduce our exposure to EMR, are going to fall far short of what we might hope. And so I felt it would be remiss of me to offer up this book without providing some pragmatic guidelines on how we might reduce this exposure. Below are some ways in which you can reduce your exposure to EMR and the other various effects of the technology that most of us our surrounded by in this modern age.

There are a lot of independent, peer reviewed studies to show that this is a real concern to be looked at, whilst there are other industry funded peer reviewed studies to suggest otherwise. While the jury is out and the stalemate remains in play, the choice is yours to decide on what action, if any, should be taken.

Below are highlighted points which will help make a major difference to how modern technology effects us, and those around us. The following steps are particularly useful to those more vulnerable in our society, such as babies, young children, young adults

(16 and under) and those that are sick.

1. Try and move away from using wireless technology and go back to using cables. It's a little inconvenient but will make a HUGE difference to you and anyone else who lives in your house/immediate space).
This means that you would;

- Turn off wifi on your internet router.
- Turn off wifi on any access point you might have around the house.
- Turn off wifi on any device that you have/use, such as a desktop computer, laptop, printer, phone, games console, tablet, iPad, smart watch, etc.
- Turn off wifi on your household appliances/devices such as a smart TV, fridge/freezer, boiler thermostat, smart meter (provided by 3rd party electricity and gas companies), portable home phone handsets (for use with landlines), security cameras, wireless speakers, etc.
- Remove and stop or limit use of any wearable technology that transmits wirelessly. These include technologies such as the wearable fitness devices available, virtual reality headsets etc.

REMEMBER – If you turn off the wireless feature on your router, but do not switch off the wireless feature on your laptop (for instance), then you are still surrounded by man-made EMR. To achieve a clear and coherent environment you will need to turn off ALL known wireless devices and transmitters in your immediate vicinity. You might not be able to turn off your neighbours wifi router, but by turning off your own routers' capability, you significantly reduce your EMR exposure to you and those around you.

2. Be smarter with your phone usage. A lot of the time, much of our communication can be sent via a text or an email rather than talking to family, friends and work colleagues for hours on end. However, sometimes it really is unavoidable. Here's some hopefully helpful tips on how you might reduce the effect of mobile phone use.

- When talking on the phone, place the phone down on a desk/table and use the loudspeaker, rather than holding the handset to your head, or using a wireless/wired headset.
- Try and send a text/instant message rather than talking to someone where possible. This isn't always possible, but you would be surprised at how often we can succinctly communicate via a brief message, rather than a protracted conversation. (Sometimes however, it may just be nice to talk to someone. Arrange to meet them face-to-face where possible).
- When carrying a phone during the day, place it in a bag or purse, rather than in a shirt or trouser pocket.
- As a default, turn off (in your handset settings) from using the 4G network on your phone where possible. It only really needs to be used when you need to access a high speed internet connection via your phone.

- Try and use a desktop computer or laptop to access the internet where possible.
- If you need to use apps and internet browsing, turn on the 4G network to complete your task and then switch it back off again after use.

3. Try and minimise your 'screen time' an hour or so before bed. This will allow the natural biorhythms of the body to settle and afford you a 'hopefully' good nights sleep.

4. Get out into a natural space such as a local park/green space or even better, somewhere out in the countryside away from large urbanised areas as often as you can. One or two days a week when possible. Even a few hours at the weekend will go some of the way in helping keep you plugged-in and attuned to the natural frequencies of nature.

5. Where possible, try and keep your sleeping environment clear from EMR. This means that you should avoid having your mobile phone, iPad, or any wireless device near you whilst you sleep. Turn off these devices - standby mode is not necessarily sufficient enough. This is particularly relevant for under 16's and those that are sick and working through an illness.

6. Keep track of and where necessary, reduce your screen time during the day/week. Find other non-hyper-stimulating things to engage with. This is

particularly relevant for under 16's and those that are sick and working through an illness.

7. Technology Free Days. Give yourself time every week (or when possible) where you do not use technology at all. Leave a message on your phone/email stating that you will not be available to communicate via these methods for the duration of your 'Free Day'. Some advocates follow the '5:2' Digital diet – 5days on, 2 days off technology.

8. Try avoid using technology during social situations to help stimulate a more engaged experience. A common thing during dinner parties/meals is 'stacking' where all at the meal will leave their turned off mobile phones/devices in a pile in the middle of the table so as to not be disturbed during their social engagement.

Why would you do any of this?

1. It will create a clear and coherent environment free from the stronger, immediate man-made EMR. This is particularly important when you go to sleep while your body gets the rest it needs.

2. By having to go to a specific place in your house to use the internet, it will help stop the habit of constantly checking for new emails and un-necessary internet usage.

3. To avoid any potential harmful effects that this

technology brings. There is much science now available to suggest that exposure to EMR does have a harmful effect upon us physiologically (recognisable changes in our DNA), mentally and emotionally (recognisable changes in brain chemistry).

4. Very recent studies show that the use of social media, and the associated technology is having a detrimental effect upon users. The same can be seen with highly-stimulating games, and 'screen time' in general.

5. It's about redefining our relationship with technology. Be really mindful of your technology use. This exercise is not meant to be a complete rejection of the use of technology, but a more intelligent approach to its use, so that we are not left being ruled by technology, but end up integrating it into our lives in a more balanced healthy way – on our terms.